BROKEN WORDS

BROKEN
WORDS

The Abuse of
Science and Faith
in American Politics

JONATHAN DUDLEY

Crown Publishers

New York

Copyright © 2011 by Jonathan Dudley

Published in the United States by Crown Publishers, an imprint of the
Crown Publishing Group, a division of Random House, Inc., New York.

www.crownpublishing.com

CROWN and the Crown colophon are registered trademarks of Random House, Inc.

Library of Congress Cataloging-in-Publication Data

Dudley, Jonathan.

Broken words: the abuse of science and faith in American politics /
by Jonathan Dudley.—1st ed.

p. cm.

Includes bibliographical references and index.

1. Evangelicalism. 2. Evangelicalism—Social aspects. 3. Church and social problems.
I. Title. II. Title: Misfortunes of science and scripture in evangelical Christian politics.

BR1640 D83 2011

261.8—dc22   2010035307

ISBN 978-0-385-52526-8

eISBN 978-0-307-72079-5

Printed in the United States of America

Book design by Leonard W. Henderson

Jacket design by Kyle Kolker

1 3 5 7 9 10 8 6 4 2

First Edition

To my parents,
who encouraged my curiosity as a child
and have graciously endured the consequences ever since

CONTENTS

So many things can be changed, being fragile as they are.
—MICHEL FOUCAULT

ONE

The Bible, Biology, and Boundaries

I LEARNED A FEW THINGS growing up as an evangelical Christian: that abortion is murder; homosexuality, sin; evolution, nonsense; and environmentalism, a farce. I learned to accept these ideas—the "big four"—as part of the package deal of Christianity. In some circles, I learned that my eternal salvation hinged on it. Those who denied them were outsiders, liberals, and legitimate targets for evangelism. If they didn't change their minds after being "witnessed to," they became legitimate targets for hell.

In this book, I explore these ideas, the "big four," from the perspective of one racked with ambivalence toward the evangelical community. Racked with ambivalence, I say, because I am emotionally attached to the evangelical culture. I grew up in it; all of my family and most of my childhood friends are from it; and I have many fond memories of singing songs at Bible camp, playing drums in my church's praise band, and reciting Bible verses in Sunday school. But I am intellectually turned off by much of the evangelical culture. Its homogeneity, politicization, naive views of biblical interpretation, embrace of pseudoscience—they all serve to turn me away. I also explore the "big four" ideas as a seminary graduate and, now, aspiring medical scientist, and one whose theological and scientific training results in a rejection of standard evangelical thought on the big four issues. This background is especially appropriate because all four topics involve the Bible and biology: Life begins at conception and terminating it before birth is murder. Homosexuality is an abomination and gays don't have to be gay. Intelligent design is the best synthesis of biochemistry with belief in God. Global warming is a myth and the earth will be destroyed when Jesus comes back anyway.

When the Bible and biology are mixed in this way, the products are boundaries. The preceding stances on each issue, in the eyes of many, define the perimeter of the evangelical community. Like walls surrounding a city, the issues serve to distinguish evangelical insiders from nonevangelical outsiders. If you don't think life begins at conception, or you believe gay marriage is OK, chances are many evangelicals won't see you as a fellow Christian. When Richard Cizik, head of the National Organization of Evangelicals, declared in 2007 he believes in human-made global warming, going counter to the views of many evangelicals, who have long insisted that global warming is a hoax, evangelical leaders demanded he resign. During the 2008 Saddleback Forum, when Barack Obama told Rick Warren he's not quite sure when life begins, his response was immediately distributed to evangelicals as proof that McCain (who told Warren that life begins at the moment of conception) was the evangelicals' candidate. When the Evangelical Lutheran Church of America voted to support gay marriage in 2009, and a tornado occurred on the same day, a leading evangelical pastor declared that God sent the tornado to punish the church. Evangelicals continue to rally around intelligent design and evince grave suspicion toward evolutionary theory. When evangelical pastor Greg Boyd wrote a book arguing that evangelicals needn't be Republicans in 2007, he lost 20 percent of his five-thousand-person congregation. The problem is not so much that evangelicals are generally Republican as that valid perspectives are squelched, while perspectives that are substantially weaker (as I will argue) are held up as defining "orthodoxy" for evangelicals.

For me, the function of these beliefs as litmus tests for Christian faith is not just an observation of the culture from afar. It is profoundly personal. I recall several stories, whispered in hushed, solemn tones after church, about the latest members who had "wandered from the faith." This often referred to supporting a pro-choice politician or accepting the theory of evolution. Assenting to the big four, on the other hand, was taken as evidence of moving *into* the faith, crossing from worldly to Christian and entering the kingdom community. A church friend once commented, "God's been working in my neighbor's heart lately." How did my friend know? Over the years the neighbor had gradually switched from supporting gay rights to opposing them.

Evangelicalism is not monolithic, nor is it stagnant. Not all evangelicals hold the "big four" views, and many evangelicals who do don't hold such views obnoxiously or uncritically. Although 78 percent of voting white evangelicals supported George W. Bush in 2004, and 74 percent supported John McCain in 2008, there is a growing politically liberal subgroup in the culture. Proenvironmentalism sentiment is increasingly common in the evangelical culture, but evangelicals are still one of the least likely groups in America—according to some polls, *the* least likely—to support the environmental movement. Though evolution-believing evangelicals such as Francis Collins—current director of the National Institutes of Health—have received support by evangelicals in some quarters, most of the culture prefers intelligent design or creation science. Rick Warren has attempted to broaden the evangelical political agenda to include issues like poverty and AIDS, but he also compares abortion to the Holocaust, and committed gay relationships to child abuse and incest. The culture may be changing—and certainly is more diverse than common stereotypes suggest—but it is still defined in ways large and small by the four issues discussed in this book.

This is a book about the Bible, biology, and boundaries. It is my personal look at four hot-button issues involving science and scripture that have assumed a central importance in defining the evangelical community. And since evangelicals constitute roughly 35 percent of Americans—and have a tremendous impact on politics—this book is about four issues that have assumed a central importance in America. Over the course of my journey through an evangelical college, a mainline seminary, and a medical school, I have concluded that evangelical thought on these topics is in need of serious critique and rethinking. But before I get to that, allow me to introduce myself and my reasons for writing this book.

I spent the first twenty years of my life in Grand Rapids, Michigan, a capital of modern evangelical Christendom. In addition to its five Christian colleges (Calvin, Cornerstone, Kuyper, Grace Bible, Aquinas), two internationally broadcast Christian radio stations, and five megachurches (including Calvary, Ada Bible, and Mars Hill Bible), Grand Rapids is also home to three of the biggest evangelical publishing companies in the world (Zondervan, Eerdmans, and Baker).

My family was similarly saturated with evangelicalism. For most of my childhood, my family attended the First Evangelical Covenant Church, where much of my time was spent memorizing Bible verses. "Hiding God's word in your heart," as it's called, is quite important in the evangelical community. And hide God's word I did—roughly two thousand verses' worth if my calculations are accurate. At the end of each year, I would recite the entire year's verses from memory for a gift certificate from my church to a local Christian bookstore. My dad wrote the Bible-memory curriculum for the church, and my mom directed the church choir and orchestra. She also conducted the choir for *Children's Bible Hour*, America's oldest Christian radio program for children.

Both of my parents, two of my grandparents, and half of my aunts and uncles attended Moody Bible Institute, a flagship fundamentalist Bible school in Chicago started by the revivalist Dwight L. Moody. In addition to requiring faculty to sign off on standard evangelical beliefs—that the Bible is inspired by God, that Jesus is divine, that one must ask Jesus into one's heart and be "born again" to attain salvation, that Christians must evangelize, that the Bible is the ultimate authority for Christians—Moody Bible Institute also requires all faculty members to reject the theory of evolution, to believe the Bible does not contain any errors about history or science, and to believe that Jesus will return at any minute to take the faithful out of this world. D. L. Moody was famous for his dismal view of society: "I look upon this world as a wrecked vessel. God has given me a lifeboat and said, 'Moody, save all you can.'"

My family regularly listened to James Dobson of Focus on the Family on the radio and received fund-raising letters from similar ministries. Both sources played a significant role in shaping our perceptions both of what the Bible says about particular issues and of the world outside our relatively homogeneous community. According to Dobson, the Bible was quite clear on whom we should vote for and what we should believe about everything ranging from foreign policy to abortion to taxes. But the outside world portrayed in his broadcasts was a scary place, populated by liberals, practicing homosexuals, and other disreputable groups—who wanted nothing more than to destroy the family, America, and Western civilization as we know it.

I have to admit from the start that, for most of my childhood, I was anything but a model Christian. As a child, I was plagued by doubts about Christianity. It all started with a children's song, from which I learned how to be saved: "If you confess with your mouth that Jesus is Lord and believe in your heart that God raised him from the dead—you will be saved!" The requirement for salvation set forth in the song was one I could never seem to meet. My eternal salvation hinged on whether or not I believed that Jesus died for my sins and was raised from the dead— whether or not, in other words, I had enough confidence that a rather improbable event occurred in ancient history. Thus, every night before bed, I would inform God in prayer that I was 100 percent sure Jesus died and was raised from the dead, and quite grateful for it as well (I made sure to conceal my doubts, thinking that if I didn't let on, God would never know). In reality, however, I was not sure that Jesus was raised from the dead, any more than I was sure about any other contested aspect of ancient history. Racked with guilt, and always fretting over my eternal destiny, I recall asking Jesus into my heart several dozen times throughout childhood—just to be safe.

Things didn't get much better in high school. My family switched churches during my time in high school (mainly because my sisters and I wanted to attend a popular megachurch with our school friends), and my mom resigned from her job as choir director to come with us. But as luck would have it, shortly after we arrived at our new church, the director of music resigned. My mom applied for the position, along with one other person. It should have been no contest. My mom had more than twenty years of experience directing church music, had obtained bachelor's and master's degrees, and was highly recommended by both her former choir and various choir members at our new church. The other applicant had little experience, did not have a master's degree, and was largely unknown to the choir. But the other applicant had one small asset that my mom lacked: a penis.

Although the church's theological position did not prevent it from hiring a woman for the role of choir director, some of the elders (all men) felt uncomfortable with such a change and pulled some strings behind the scenes to ensure that the male candidate was hired (as a member of the board later confessed). And although several friends in law told us it was a clear-cut case of gender discrimination that invited a lawsuit, my parents did not want to tarnish the church's reputation. The older male in charge of hiring called my mom into his office to offer a bizarre, tearful apology, then sent her off "in the name of the Lord" to keep quiet about what had happened.

That soured me quite a bit on evangelical Christianity and also taught me that the Lord's name can be used to support just about anything—sexism, bigotry, anti-intellectualism, you name it. (Although unqualified for the job of choir director at our local church, my mom went on to graduate summa cum laude from a doctoral program in choral conducting and now directs a choir and teaches music at a university.)

Although I kept going to the church, things went downhill throughout high school. The church youth group would frequently host speakers I could relate to, people like me, who could never seem to get the Christian thing right: shooting heroin, having unprotected sex with everyone in sight, and generally making the worst possible decision in every situation. But at the end of each story—each of which utterly captivated me—while lying in a jail cell or a pool of vomit or standing on the edge of a bridge getting ready to jump, it would happen. The narrator would give his life to Jesus and enter a personal relationship with God. These former drug users, school dropouts, and sex addicts were the heroes of our culture, the main speakers at our most important events. Having this route to spiritual satisfaction inscribed in my subconscious, and very much wanting to achieve herohood among my peers, I set out in high school to destroy my life as utterly and comprehensively as possible.

Fortunately, I didn't succeed. I did smoke marijuana a few times, watched R-rated movies with friends, and during a moment of utter abandon, used the "F-word" in front of my dad, but for some reason, perhaps because I was so thoroughly shaped by evangelical morality, I couldn't bring myself to enact more damage upon my life. I resigned myself to face the fact that my testimony would never be as cool as those of the youth group speakers—if I ever had one, that is.

But as it turns out, I would have a testimony. It all started my senior year of high school, when I worked out a deal with my dad to get out of going to Sunday school. Rather than suffering through the well-meaning but painful antics of a middle-aged youth pastor ("PRAISE THE NAME OF JESUS!!!!!!" he would yell several times throughout the service, with sweat dripping down his balding head, to which everyone would yell "YEAH!!!" or "You know it!"), I would stay at home and read books about theology and Christianity. I started off reading arguments for and against Christianity and then continued on to read about theology, Christian history, and ethics. To my surprise, there were quite a few smart people in the Christian tradition and many of their arguments were convincing. Although I wasn't convinced that Christianity is true, I was at least convinced that it wasn't irrational. And I think that's about as far as you can get with arguments for a particular religious perspective anyway.

That summer I decided to go on a ten-week mission trip to Europe with my church. Mostly, I just wanted to see Europe. But in the training camp before the trip, where we memorized the Four Spiritual Laws (a tract summarizing how to be saved), practiced evangelism, and learned street theater skits to present the Gospel message, something unexpected happened. I asked Jesus into my heart for what was probably the six dozenth time, and I was born again (again). But for real this time. Many evangelicals will describe their conversion experience as follows: "I came to a realization of my sinfulness, my need for forgiveness and Jesus as Savior, and began a personal relationship with God." Many people, including me, find such rhetoric mostly opaque. But somewhere in those words, struggling to get out, is an ineffable experience of something more, of grace, second chances, and regeneration. And all who've experienced it know exactly what that means. In my case, it meant I began praying every day, reading my Bible more often, attempting to cultivate the virtues I saw in scripture, and trying harder in school.

Then it was off to college—I majored in biology at Calvin College—and off to a series of intellectual experiences that eventually led to this book. Since most of my teen years were spent rebelling against my parents and their beliefs, I wasn't as firmly wedded to "the big four" positions as many of my evangelical peers. Although I went to an evangelical college—as happens in many evangelical homes, it was either that or my parents wouldn't pay—I nevertheless encountered strong opposition to many pop-culture evangelical beliefs. In my freshman biology class, I sat riveted as the professor explained why scientists believe in evolution (I had never learned about the subject in high school). The summer after my first year, I pored over a summer-school psychology book by an evangelical professor, who argued (shockingly, to me) that gay people don't choose their orientation and cannot readily change. Over the course of my second year in college, I learned why scientists think there is an environmental crisis. And during my last year of college, a bioethics professor argued against popular evangelical thought on abortion. I was surprised to find out during an office visit that many other evangelical scholars shared his view, though not surprised when he said they would rather not speak up about it due to the avalanche of protests it would generate from college donors. These conclusions were reaffirmed during my seminary studies at Yale, where I also learned to appreciate mainline Christian thought, which often reaches a degree of nuance and sophistication seldom encountered in evangelicalism.

Nevertheless, my bioethics professor reinforced a conclusion I had drawn from my undergrad and seminary years: There is a significant gap between the opinions that dominate the popular evangelical culture (which is the only part of evangelicalism with political muscle) and the opinions that prevail among leading evangelical scholars. This gap has huge political consequences. If lay evangelical opinion reflected scholarly evangelical opinion—or, better yet, the outcome of serious dialogue between evangelical and mainline Christian scholars—instead of the opinions of radio broadcasters and televangelists, American politics would look very different indeed. It would be infused with more moderation, less partisanship, more willingness to compromise. Political debates would focus less on questioning established science—on whether global warming is real, for example—and more on the proper response to established science. Faith would inform both the Right and the Left.

Over the past decade, there have been numerous calls from the secular world for religion to stay out of politics. The separation of church and state, we learn, means that religious people should bracket their convictions when entering the voting booth, lobbying representatives and senators, and certainly while constructing public policies. Those who advocate religion-free politics in the face of the evangelical Right, however, rarely bemoan the influence of Rev. Martin Luther King Jr. in the civil rights movement or of progressive evangelicals today in the environmental movement. Ross Douthat, a *New York Times* columnist, laments this apparent inconsistency: "A Christian is allowed to . . . mix religion and politics in support of sweeping social reforms—but only if those reforms are safely identified with the political Left, and the interests of the Democratic party." Perhaps the problem is not so much that faith and politics mix, but the quality of religious thought, especially evangelical thought, that is brought into the political arena.

And over the past several decades, the quality of evangelical thought has been sorely wanting. As historian Mark Noll writes in his book *The Scandal of the Evangelical Mind*, "The scandal of the evangelical mind is that there is not much of an evangelical mind. . . . American evangelicals are not exemplary for their thinking, and they have not been so for several generations." Noll elaborates:

> They have nourished millions of believers in the simple
> verities of the gospel but have largely abandoned
> the universities. . . . Evangelicals sponsor dozens of
> theological seminaries, scores of colleges, hundreds
> of radio stations, and thousands of unbelievably
> diverse parachurch agencies—but not a single
> research university or a single periodical devoted
> to in-depth interaction with modern culture. . . .
> *Christianity Today* [the leading evangelical periodical in
> America], which, for a decade or so after its founding
> in 1956, aspired to intellectual leadership, has been

transformed into a journal of news and middle-brow religious commentary in order simply to stay in business. . . . Evangelicals spend enormous sums on higher education, but the diffusion of resources among hundreds of colleges and seminaries means that almost none can begin to afford a research faculty, theological or otherwise.

The evangelical community, he explains, does not generally produce the books that revolutionize our thinking about the world, does not make the scientific discoveries that earn Nobel Prizes, and does not support the people who do. In fact, the evangelical culture has tended to squelch new ideas by prizing conformity and granting more weight to the opinions of popular leaders than those of scholars and intellectuals. Noll is no narrow-minded opponent of all things evangelical. He published these words during his twenty-seven-year tenure at Wheaton College (he is currently at Notre Dame), widely considered the leading evangelical college in America, and his book won the Book-of-the-Year award from *Christianity Today*. His sentiments are shared by many.

One manifestation of Noll's *Scandal of the Evangelical Mind* is a high level of certainty among many evangelicals that their views—and theirs alone—are the correct ones. As Notre Dame sociologist Christian Smith observes in his book *American Evangelicalism*: "American evangelicals believe not only that an unchanging and universal Truth exists, but—more audaciously, perhaps—that *they* are the ones who know it." Smith arrives at his conclusions both from a survey of evangelical history and from interviews with hundreds of evangelicals across America. "We as Christians have to understand that we have the answer," was a frequent comment made by interviewees. After summarizing several polls, Georgetown political scientist Clyde Wilcox makes a similar observation in his book *Onward Christian Soldiers?*:

Although religious liberals and secularists may
believe that all voices should be heard and tested in
the marketplace of ideas, fundamentalists and other
evangelicals believe that they already have the inerrant
truth and that other ideas are simply wrong.

This mind-set extends not only to what most would consider core elements of Christian orthodoxy—the divine nature of scripture, the deity of Jesus, the existence of a triune God—which one could hardly blame those who call themselves Christians for being confident about. It also extends to policy positions, the interpretation of contested passages of the Bible, disputes over controversial aspects of science and history, philosophical theories, and a host of other such issues.

This extreme certainty among evangelicals that "we have the Truth" inspires uncompromising political activism on behalf of positions that—due to the weakness of evangelical thought for several generations—have not always been carefully thought through. And the combination of these two features—put bluntly, ignorance and arrogance—understandably irks the broader culture. Perhaps that's why, as *New York Times* columnist Nicholas Kristof has observed, "Christian evangelicals . . . constitute one of the few minorities that, on the American coasts or university campuses, it remains fashionable to mock." The poverty of evangelical thinking, combined with "we have the Truth" political activism, is understandably off-putting to many.

How does this relate to the four issues discussed in this book? Widespread belief among evangelicals that abortion is murder from conception onward has wedded evangelicals firmly and uncritically to the Republican Party. It has also made parochial politics inevitable. Because what other issues can compare to mass murder taking place in your own country? Naive views about biblical interpretation, which hold that we can derive our political positions and theology from a simple, lens-free reading of scripture, have led evangelicals—on both the right and the left—to ignore the theology and politics that already guide their readings of scripture. This has led evangelicals to ethnocentrism, to asserting their historically contingent cultural values as "biblical truth." In the conservative direction, this has closed off productive dialogue between evangelicals and mainline Christians on gay marriage—because if the Bible has an obvious stance on the matter, as most evangelicals believe, the other side must be intentionally denying the truth. In the liberal direction, this has led green evangelicals to ignore the role contemporary experiences and theology have played in their reinterpretation of the Bible on environmental matters. Indeed, the use of scripture by the evangelical Left is often just as politicized and tendentious as that by the evangelical Right. Finally, the widespread rejection of evolution among evangelicals has fed into a rejection of science whenever it has implications evangelicals don't like. Because if the entire scientific community is wrong about evolution, then they're probably not worth trusting on global warming, the science of homosexuality, stem cells, or other politically charged matters. Granted, scientists are not without biases, and Christians may have different assumptions that lead them to interpret data differently. But evangelicals will regularly reject a mainstream scientific position, not because the evidence is wanting or because Christian theology requires it, but because they don't like its political implications.

I realized during the course of studying biology in undergrad and ethics in seminary that there are serious challenges to evangelical thought on all these issues—abortion, gay marriage, environmentalism, and evolution. What's more, I realized they have not been aired, in large part, because those most qualified to air them fear the popular evangelical outrage that often results from airing such grievances. Many of those who are equipped to publicly counter popular evangelical thought on these topics do not do so because they are employed by evangelical churches, colleges, parachurch organizations, or seminaries and would like to keep their jobs, or at least reputations. I realized that I was in a unique position to dispute evangelical thought on these matters given my scientific training and seminary education (I focused on bioethics). I realized it was time to speak up. The thesis of the book is simple: Evangelicalism has defined itself by weakly supported boundary markers, which are justified by a flawed understanding of biblical interpretation and maintained by suppressing those who disagree. Further, this fact has significant implications for American politics.

A story is told about a pastor who was in the midst of a sermon when a breeze entered the room and blew his notes to the floor. As a congregant helped gather the papers, she saw in one of the margins: "weak point → yell like hell!" My purpose in this book is to demonstrate that the big four conclusions are weak points. And I will argue, against current evangelical tendencies, that the proper response is not "yell like hell!" Because I learned a few other things growing up as an evangelical Christian: that all truth belongs to God, that God created the natural world, that God cares about social minorities and outcasts, and that all humans are finite and prone to err. And I'd like to see those beliefs—not the big four—once again define the evangelical community.

TWO

Pro-Life Proselytizing:
Abortion, Stem Cells, and the Moment of Conception

"How could anyone vote for a Democrat?"

I heard the question frequently growing up. I often asked it myself. When my Calvin College roommate told me he was thinking of voting for John Kerry in 2004, my respect for him immediately plummeted. I simply could no longer regard him as a serious Christian and felt compelled by my faith to convince him to vote for George W. Bush. No serious Christian could vote for a Democrat where I come from.

Democrats support murdering babies.

"Make no mistake about it," one Talbot Theological Seminary professor has declared, "abortion is killing babies. . . . If you choose to have an abortion, you are killing your son or daughter." And when the other candidate supports killing babies, the question of who to vote for is pretty much settled. Naturally, this seminary professor instructs those in his church to "vote for elected officials based on their pro-life stance." Likewise, Rick Warren of *Purpose Driven Life* fame compares abortion to the Holocaust and calls it a nonnegotiable issue for Christians in voting decisions.

You needn't stray far into the world of evangelicalism to discover that this is the prime reason for its union with the Republican Party—and its simultaneous exclusion of all things (and people) to the left. A regular contributor for *Christianity Today* responded in a 2007 column with incredulity to a small group of politically liberal evangelicals who were weary of seeing their faith so intimately linked to the Republican Party: "If you are tired of talking about the 50 million unborn human beings lost to abortion since 1973, then you know which lever to pull. How we vote as Christians may differ, and that's okay." In other words, if you don't care about genocide, vote Democrat. Just stop giving us Christians trouble for voting Republican. (Politically liberal evangelicals generally consider themselves "pro-life" and agree with conservatives on the immorality of abortion but nevertheless think it should not be the only, or even the main, item on the political agenda of evangelicals. This belief leads them to vote Democrat most of the time.) The magazine, which is the biggest, oldest, and most important evangelical magazine in America, later invited a representative of the group (Jim Wallis) for an interview, in which it raked him over the coals for supporting pro-choice Democrats. A few pages later, just to make sure there was no confusion, a contributor reaffirmed that commitment to electing pro-life candidates should still be the defining feature of evangelical politics.

Christianity Today's response to Wallis is understandable. Frankly, politically liberal evangelicals don't have a coherent position on this issue. They generally agree with, or at least leave unchallenged, the logic underlying evangelical opposition to abortion. And thus, their pleas to "expand the issue agenda" don't quite make sense: "Abortion may be morally equivalent to government-sponsored baby genocide," they seem to be saying, "but we should also care about recycling and improving public schools." Even when you weigh abortion against issues like war and capital punishment, there is still no contest; at most, a few thousand lives are lost by US-led wars and capital punishment every year. A few thousand abortions are performed every day. Imagine Dietrich Bonhoeffer in Nazi Germany, berating fellow Christians for letting the Holocaust distract them from environmental or economic concerns.

If you believe, as most evangelicals do, that abortion is killing babies at any stage of pregnancy, there's little room for compromise. In this light, most of the popular pro-choice arguments fail. We may live in a pluralistic society. It may be incumbent on society to respect women's privacy. And it may be practically impossible to enforce a prohibition on abortion. But none of that really matters if abortion entails killing innocent humans. As ethicist Lew Smedes rightly notes, "A pluralist society does not allow people to follow their consciences if their consciences lead them to kill an innocent human being. A free society will invade a person's privacy if it is certain that she is privately about to kill an innocent human being. A wise society may well make laws it does not have the will to enforce if not to pass them makes killing human beings legal."

Given the widespread and intense conviction among evangelicals—on both the left and the right—that life begins at conception and abortion is killing an innocent human being from then on, you'd think this position is clearly taught in the Bible, the mainstream position of historic Christianity, or firmly established by modern science.

You'd be wrong.

The Bible

"The reason I believe life begins at conception is 'cause the Bible says it," declares Rick Warren in a 2008 interview. Warren's beliefs about the Bible are common in the evangelical community. As mentioned earlier, when then-presidential-candidate Barack Obama told Warren during the 2008 election season that the question of when life begins is "above my pay grade" (versus John McCain's answer that life begins "at the moment of conception"), the two responses were quickly disseminated to the evangelical community as proof that McCain was the evangelicals' candidate. And the main reason most evangelicals believe life begins at conception, in their minds at least, is because the Bible says so.

Focus on the Family claims in its literature to provide "Scripture verses that speak to the value of preborn life created in God's image from the moment of fertilization." Here is an example of Focus on the Family's exegesis, found in a section of their website titled "What the Bible Says About the Beginning of Life." Under a section titled "Q. Are the Preborn Human Beings?," the authors answer by declaring "The Lord Jesus Christ began his incarnation as an embryo, growing into a fetus, infant, child, teenager, and adult." Their sole cited support for this conclusion about the moment of the incarnation is Luke 2:6–7 (NIV): "While they were there, the time came for the baby to be born, and she gave birth to her firstborn, a son."

The second and final verse Focus on the Family uses to establish that fetal personhood begins at fertilization is Luke 1:41, 44 (NIV): "When Elizabeth heard Mary's greeting, the baby leaped in her womb, and Elizabeth was filled with the Holy Spirit . . . [saying] 'As soon as the sound of your greeting reached my ears, the baby in my womb leaped for joy.'" The implicit suggestion that this verse provides us with information on when moral life begins (along with the interpretations of Psalm 139 and Jeremiah 1, discussed later) reflects the willingness—evidenced also in the creationist movement—of modern, populist evangelicalism to interpret any part of the Bible, including its poetry and narratives, as conveying precise factual information about contemporary moral and scientific issues.

The Southern Baptist Convention has also promoted the idea that the Bible teaches that life begins at conception. In its resolution against human embryonic stem cell research, it declared: "The Bible teaches that human beings are made in the image and likeness of God (Gen. 1:27; 9:6) and protectable human life begins at fertilization." The wording is tricky; does the Bible teach that human beings are made in the image of God *and* that protectable human life begins at fertilization? Or is the second part of the sentence simply a naked assertion tacked on to the first? The verses cited have nothing to do with when life begins. They include Genesis 1:27, "So God created humankind in his image, in the image of God he created them; male and female he created them," and Genesis 9:6, "Whoever sheds the blood of a human by a human shall that person's blood be shed; for in his own image God made humankind." From both verses, we might conclude that humans are created in the image of God and for that reason, it is wrong to kill humans. But this does not tell us whether the fertilized egg should be considered and treated as a "human." There is no logical path from the belief that humans are created in the image of God to the conclusion that the embryo, therefore, is a human created in the image of God.

Another common interpretation, used by Focus on the Family and a number of other organizations, is simply to cite Exodus 20:13's "Thou shalt not murder" and then conclude that settles the matter. Here we find the same type of circular reasoning witnessed above. Just as the fact that humans are created in the image of God does not tell us whether the embryo is a human, the fact that murder is wrong does not tell us whether taking the life of an early embryo is murder. Those who support abortion do not generally believe it is murder.

Several verses can be interpreted as speaking with reverence of fetal life. Psalm 139:13, 16 says, "For it was you who formed me in my inward parts; you knit me together in my mother's womb. . . . Your eyes beheld my unformed substance. In your book were written all the days that were formed for me, when none of them as yet existed." Jeremiah 1:5 declares, "Before I formed you in the womb, I knew you, and before you were born I consecrated you; I appointed you a prophet to the nations." And in Ephesians 1:4, we read, "God chose us in Him before the creation of the world."

Some commentators have concluded that these verses tell us that fetal personhood begins at conception, or at least before birth. But these pieces of poetry can just as readily be interpreted as dealing with God's foreknowledge, not with when personhood begins. After all, the psalmist speaks of God's knowledge of all his days "when none of them as yet existed." Jeremiah also begins with "before I formed you in the womb."

If these verses tell us when personhood begins, shouldn't we rather conclude that it begins *before* conception? Or better, as Ephesians 1:4 has it,
"before the creation of the world"? As one biblical scholar puts it: "God
knows and calls us not just from the time of conception but even *before*
conception—even from before the foundation of the world."

An additional problem with this interpretation is that all of the
passages are written from the perspective of a fully developed person
looking back and affirming that God has always had a plan for his or
her life. When we take the perspective of an embryo looking forward,
the situation changes dramatically; due to genetic anomalies, hormone
imbalances, and a number of unknown factors, more than half of all embryos are spontaneously miscarried before implanting in the uterus. In
light of this fact, many Christian theologians—including, for example,
the Catholic Saint Anselm and the theologian Karl Rahner—have found it
incompatible with their understanding of God to hold the belief that the
majority of people God brings into being achieve less biological complexity than a sunflower seed.

In sum, we must conclude that the Bible is much less helpful on the
question of when moral life begins and whether abortion is murder than
many politically conservative evangelicals would like us to believe. Even
many scholars who staunchly oppose abortion admit as much. Willem A.
VanGemeren, a professor of Old Testament at Trinity Evangelical Divinity School and an opponent of abortion, admits of the Bible that "nothing
addresses abortion directly." Richard B. Hays, a professor of New Testament at Duke University, believes Christians should oppose abortion but
nevertheless can state: "The Bible contains no texts about abortion. This
simple fact—often ignored by those who would make opposition to abortion into a virtual litmus text of true Christian faith—places the issue of
abortion in a very different category." Pope John Paul II, despite having
led one of the most intense campaigns against abortion in the history
of the Church, nevertheless believed that "the texts of Sacred Scripture

never address the question of deliberate abortion and so do not directly and specifically condemn it."

Despite these concessions by antiabortion thinkers, the Bible has played some role in historic Christian thought on abortion. The one verse that has consistently come to the fore in past theological discussions, not yet mentioned, is Exodus 21:22–25. The New Revised Standard Version reads: "When men have a fight and hurt a pregnant woman, so that she suffers a miscarriage, but no further injury, the guilty one shall be fined as much as the woman's husband demands of him, and he shall pay in the presence of judges. But if injury ensues, you shall give life for life." Here, the accidental destruction of fetal life requires a fine while harm to the mother requires "life for life," suggesting a difference in the moral status of fetal versus maternal life. Granted, there are some ambiguities in the ancient manuscript that keep this conclusion from being certain. Nevertheless, the passage was taken throughout history, in both the Jewish and Christian traditions, as a basis for elevating the life of the mother over that of the fetus.

Judaism

Since pro-life evangelicals often claim to be representing Judeo-Christian values in their campaign against abortion, it will be informative to examine what Jews believe about the matter. And indeed, most of the verses used to support the "life begins at conception" position are located in a portion of the Bible that Christians share with Jews—the Old Testament, or Hebrew Bible. Orthodox Judaism is famous for the rigor and devotion with which its adherents approach scripture. In Jesus's day, and in many Jewish communities to the present, children will have memorized the first five books of the Bible—Genesis, Exodus, Leviticus, Numbers, and Deuteronomy—by their tenth birthday. The better students went on to memorize the remaining thirty-four books of the Hebrew Bible by the time they turn fourteen. Through several millennia, Jews have reflected on the Hebrew Bible and recorded their interpretations and discussions in Talmud (a collection of commentaries on ethics, law, and theology that is central to the Jewish faith). With all this intense engagement with scripture, what do Jews think the Bible says about fetal life?

Jews think the Bible says life begins at birth. This position is justified based on the Exodus 21 passage cited above and also Genesis 2:7, in which Adam's life begins when he acquires the ability to breathe. Since the first breaths are taken at birth, full moral status is acquired then as well. Thus, if the mother is having difficulty during pregnancy, late-term abortion is commanded by the Talmud. As the Mishna, a core portion of the Talmud, states:

> If a woman has difficulty in childbirth, one dismembers
> the embryo within her limb from limb because her life
> takes precedence over its life. Once its head (or the
> greater part) has emerged, it may not be touched, for
> we do not set aside one life for another.

Because the fetus is not considered to have the moral status of an independently living person, when a Jewish woman has a miscarriage, the burial of the fetus is not surrounded by religious ritual, and indeed, does not even take place in a cemetery. These beliefs allow some Jews to recommend abortion in other cases as well: If the mother may go deaf by carrying the fetus to term, the fetus may be deformed, or the pregnancy may bring the mother disgrace.

These beliefs are not merely a thing of the past, made irrelevant by modern scientific or moral thinking. They persist within Judaism to this day. Hence, at the beginning of former president George W. Bush's tenure, Orthodox Jews issued a statement supporting human embryonic stem cell research:

> Our Torah [the first five books of the Christian Old
> Testament] places great value upon human life . . .
> each human was created in God's image. . . . The
> Torah commands us to treat and cure the ill and to
> defeat disease wherever possible; to do this is to be the
> Creator's partner in safeguarding the created. . . .
> [M]aximizing the potential to save and heal human lives
> is an integral part of valuing human life. Moreover,
> our tradition states that an embryo in vitro does not
> enjoy the full status of human-hood and its attendant
> protections. Thus, if cloning technology research
> advances our ability to heal humans with greater
> success, it ought to be pursued.

What the Jewish community demonstrates, with its long tradition of respecting humans as made in God's image, is that it is consistent to think human life is immeasurably valuable and also think it begins later than conception. The question of when moral life begins is a question of how far back the category "human" should extend; the question of the value of human life is a question of how what is already placed in the category "human" should be treated. The mistake many evangelicals make is to conflate the two questions.

The evangelical Right has a very broad category of "human," with a full moral status granted to the earliest embryo, but it does not treat what it puts in that category very well. To accuse the Right of believing that life begins at conception and ends at birth may be hyperbole, but it does have a ring of truth. According to some polls, the most likely group in America to support war, capital punishment, and state-sponsored torture of political prisoners is also the most likely to identify as "pro-life." The 2004 National Election Study poll, for example, found that of mainline Protestants, evangelical Protestants, Catholics, and members of other religious groups, evangelicals were most likely to believe abortion is never permissible (25 percent), to oppose government funding of abortion (75 percent), and to favor a ban on partial birth abortion (76 percent), but were also the most likely of the four groups to strongly favor the death penalty (61 percent) and to support the war in Iraq (58 percent). In 2002, Charles Colson, who declares his opposition to abortion flows out of his high respect for human life, teamed up with the fervently pro-life Richard Land of the Southern Baptist Convention to write a letter telling George W. Bush that a preemptive war against Iraq could be theologically justified. In *Christianity Today*, Colson wrote, "Sometimes going to war is the charitable thing to do." Today's Religious Right leaders either opposed or ignored the civil rights movement and have actively campaigned against the feminist movement. Jerry Falwell and Pat Robertson blamed September 11, in part, on feminists.

Some may argue that supporting war and capital punishment, and opposing aid for the economically and socially oppressed, have no self-evident relationship to one's overall view of human life. If that is true in those cases, it is even more true when it comes to abortion. War, capital punishment, and the like deal with how we treat entities we all place in the category "human." Abortion, at least for many participants in the debate, deals with what counts as "human" in the first place. If you don't think abortion kills humans, you reveal nothing about your respect for humans by supporting it.

In any case, it is highly ironic that politically conservative evangelicals claim to be representing "Judeo-Christian values." Their abortion policies would make it illegal for Jews to obey some portions of the Talmud.

Christian Tradition

If pro-life evangelicals are not representing "the Judeo-Christian tradi-tion" in their campaign against abortion, surely, at least, they must be representing the Christian tradition. After all, this is the group that gen-erally insists, in its campaign against homosexuality, on how important it is to them to uphold "the traditional interpretation of the Bible." Surely, Christians throughout history must have interpreted the Bible as teaching that life begins at conception and abortion is murder.

In fact, although some early Christians, such as the writers of *The Didache*, Tertullian and Basil, and John Calvin did think abortion kills a person from conception, and occasionally used the Bible to support their views (though Tertullian's position was condemned as heresy, and Cal-vin's, articulated only in passing, was abandoned by most of the Protes-tants who followed him), the dominant view in Christian tradition has been that moral life begins when the body acquires a human form, rudi-mentary organs, and/or substantial brain activity. Abortions performed prior to that point are viewed as morally equivalent to using contracep-tion. Though contraceptive use was a grave sin for pre-Reformation Christians, even on par with murder—and, in the eyes of some theolo-gians, worse—it is not a sin for most evangelicals today. In considering the history of Christian thought on abortion, it is important to consider the thought of Augustine and Aquinas, who articulated the mainstream Christian position before the split between Protestantism and Catholi-cism, and of later Catholic theologians, who set the stage for evangelical views today.

Early Christian views on when the soul is united with the human body (a process known as "ensoulment") were formulated over and against the dualism of matter and spirit postulated by Plato. Plato taught that humans are fundamentally a duality of soul and body, with the two parts merely brought together, not integrated. In Plato's analysis, the soul needn't have any logical relationship to what it inhabits, and thus, can exist in any material entity whatsoever. In this analysis, a human soul could inhabit, for example, a car or a turtle. It could even inhabit a single cell.

Most early Christian theologians, in contrast, believed (following Aristotle) that the human person is a fully integrated unity. Because of this, they believed that the soul must have a logical relationship to what it inhabits. The soul cannot enter any material entity, in this analysis, like a tenant might enter any number of apartments. Instead, rather than entering a material entity, the soul is united with it, and the soul can only be united with material entities bearing a particular form. The soul and the body are like two sides of the same coin, like the relationship between an apartment and its shape. The soul can't come into existence without a body. Therefore, although these theologians believed the entity created at conception was alive and biologically human, they did not believe it could receive a human soul, also known as an "intellectual soul," until it acquired both the shape of a human body and the organs required for spiritual activities, such as the brain and nervous system. This doctrine became known as *hylomorphism*. The late Joseph Donceel, a philosophical theologian from Fordham University, explained it thus: "If form and matter are strictly complementary, as hylomorphism holds, there can be an actual human soul only in a body endowed with the organs required for the spiritual activities of man. We know that the brain, and especially the cortex, are the main organs of those highest sense activities without which no spiritual activity is possible." In other words: no brain, no soul.

Many modern medical practices reflect this idea. Death is legally defined as the cessation of brain activity. Anencephalic infants, babies born without a functional brain, have heads shrunken like tennis balls and/or filled with fluid; the standard and uncontroversial practice is to allow their bodies to die. Occasionally, the embryo does not go on to form a fetus, but becomes what doctors call a "hydatidaform mole," a disorganized mass of tissue growing in the uterus. Whereas Plato would have no problem considering this tumor to be an ensouled human person, Aristotle and the Christian theologians who followed him would not view this as an ensouled human—even though it is human life bearing a unique set of chromosomes—because it has neither human form nor the organs necessary for intellectual activity.

Although an in-depth exposition of hylomorphism would have to wait until Thomas Aquinas came along during the medieval era, the beginnings of the idea can be found in the early church fathers. Therefore, although he admitted some uncertainty on the matter, Augustine nevertheless wrote:

> If what is brought forth is unformed but at this stage
> some sort of living, shapeless thing . . . then the law
> of homicide would not apply, for it could not be said
> that there was a living soul in that body, for it lacks all
> sense, if it be such as is not yet formed and therefore
> not yet endowed with senses.

Augustine—who identified the image of God in humans as "reason or mind or intelligence"—was followed by other church fathers. Jerome, for example, wrote, "Seeds are gradually formed in the uterus, and it is not reputed homicide until the scattered elements receive their appearance and members." Gregory of Nyssa declared: "It would not be possible to style the unformed embryo a human being, but only a potential one—assuming that it is completed so as to come forth to human birth, while so long as it is in this unformed state it is something other than a human." Gennadius of Marseille opined, "The soul is infused and created after the body has already been formed." Ambrosiaster, a disciple of Augustine, also expressed the now orthodox view, justifying his views with reference to both Exodus 21 and the Genesis account of God creating Adam. Anselm, a Catholic saint and theologian of the Middle Ages, affirmed that "no human intellect accepts the view that an infant has a rational soul from the moment of conception." Apparently, all of these skilled biblical interpreters found no reason to abandon their views when they read King David's account of God knitting him together in his mother's womb or the Gospel of Luke's statement that John the Baptist leaped in the womb when Mary approached bearing Jesus.

Perhaps the most sustained and thorough treatment of ensoulment in church history was that of Thomas Aquinas, a systematic theologian and doctor of the church. Aquinas's biggest accomplishment was in reconciling Christianity with Aristotelian thought, which represented the best science and philosophy of his day. Though previous theologians had drawn on the philosopher, Aquinas's engagement was at a much more detailed level. Following Aristotle, Aquinas believed that the embryo goes through a number of early stages in which—although it is alive and biologically human—it does not have the shape of a human, nor a developed brain. This led him to conclude that, because a soul can only be united with a body capable of performing spiritual activities, the soul could not possibly be united with the body until at least forty days after conception (he got the number from Aristotelian science). As Aquinas states, "[T]he rational soul ought to be united to a body which may be a suitable organ of sensation . . . before the body has organs in any way whatever, it cannot be receptive of the soul."

Aquinas's biology here is mostly correct by today's standards; the embryo does not have the form of a human body throughout pregnancy. Where Aquinas went wrong was in his belief that the fetus had a brain sufficiently developed to support sentient intellectual life after only forty days of development. Today, we know that the rudimentary organs are not developed until around ten weeks after conception and that the brain is not sufficiently developed to support sentient intellectual life until around six months after conception.

Aquinas's views, which clarified the logic of the view held since Augustine, were widely embraced in the broader culture, remained the official view of the church until the mid-1800s, and have persisted among theologians to the present day. The Italian literary figure Dante took up Aquinas's views in his poetry. In the *Divine Comedy*, he notes: ". . . so soon as in the embryo the fitting of the brain is perfected, the first Mover turns him to it, with joy over such art of nature, and breathes a new spirit." The famous surgeon Thomas Vicary (1490–1561) also affirmed the standard medieval view, asserting in Old English: "The fourth and laste, as when al the other members be perfectly shapen, then it receyeth the soule with life and breath; and then it beginneth to move it-selfe alone. . . . So is there xlvj [forty] dayes from the day of conception vnto the day of ful perfection and receyuing of the soule, as God best knoweth." The Roman Ritual, in a set of guidelines for priests (in force from 1617 to 1895), states that fetuses protruding from the womb prematurely should only be baptized after quickening (when they are felt to move inside the mother). Alphonsus Liguori, a canonized doctor of the Church, summed things up thus: "[N]ot every lump of flesh should be baptized which lacks every arrangement of organs, since it is universally accepted that the soul is not infused into the body before the latter is formed."

The Roman Catholic Church officially changed its position in the mid-1800s, due to revisions in teaching about Mary; widespread belief among scientists and theologians that the human sperm contains a fully developed, miniature human (called a "homunculus"), with a brain equipped to receive a soul at conception; and a resurgence of Platonism in Christian understandings of human identity. Nevertheless, many theologians maintained the position that the soul is infused at some point during gestation. A Catholic theologian named H. M. Hering investigated in the mid-1900s whether theologians had given up the theory of delayed ensoulment as incompatible with modern scientific and philosophical thought. He found the opposite true: While the theory was less prevalent among "the moralists and the canonists," many of whom had abandoned it in the late 1800s, "St. Thomas' doctrine in this domain is accepted by many," he noted, especially among philosophers and scholars conversant with modern biological knowledge. Contemporary defenders of some form of the position that the body is united with a soul during pregnancy have included Margaret Farley of Yale University, Joseph Donceel of Fordham University, and Karl Rahner, one of the leading Catholic scholars of the 1900s.

Evangelical Tradition

The evangelical Right often notes how much influence Protestant Christians had in the laws and government of early America. Therefore, we might expect the earliest abortion laws to reflect Christian values. And in fact, they do. Consistent with the long stream of theological thought before them, the first laws in America allowed abortion right up to around the fifth month after conception at the time of quickening, when the fetus moves in the mother's womb and, according to some theologians, the developing body is united with the human soul. Thus, James Wilson, one of the signatories of the Declaration of Independence and US Constitution, could write, summarizing early American legal practice: "In the contemplation of law, life begins when the infant is first able to stir in the womb."

Consistent with this view, abortion was practiced among Protestant Christians at the time. Several nineteenth-century doctors noted that "otherwise quite intelligent and refined [women], with a keen sense of their moral and religious obligations to themselves and to others, deem it nothing amiss to destroy the embryo during the first few months of its growth." Due to the high number of abortions sought by his Protestant patients, one doctor worried that "the Puritanic blood of '76 will be but sparingly represented in the approaching centenary."

When around the mid-1800s medical advances began making direct abortion safer, the main partakers were married Protestant women. As James Mohr notes, in his seminal history *Abortion in America*, "Most observers, then, agreed that most of the women who drove America's abortion rates so steeply upward after 1840 were married. Most observers also agreed that virtually all of the women who sought abortions in the United States during the middle decades of the nineteenth century share at least one other characteristic: They appeared to be almost exclusively Protestant." Indeed, the prevalence of abortion among Protestant women (versus mostly immigrant Catholics) is widely considered by historians to be one of the main reasons that physicians, worried that immigrant Catholics were outreproducing their mainly Protestant social group, led the campaign to criminalize abortions in the late 1800s. Other reasons cited include an upsurge in belief among physicians that the embryo is human life with a full moral status throughout pregnancy, a reaction to the campaign for female equality, concerns about the safety of the abortion procedure, and an attempt to consolidate control of medical practice.

Nevertheless, given the relatively tolerant views of early abortion within Protestant Christianity, the evangelical faith, unlike the nineteenth-century medical establishment, did not play a role in America's first campaign to outlaw abortion. Although late-nineteenth-century evangelicalism most certainly motivated other political campaigns—the abolition of slavery, movement for female equality, reform of prisons, and outlawing of alcohol—it did not take part in the campaign to criminalize abortion. As Tim Stafford laments in the now officially pro-life *Christianity Today*, "Protestant clergy had considerable prestige and were important in other reform movements of the time—notably temperance—but to the dismay of doctors, most churches ignored the issue." America's first anti-abortion laws were thus passed in the late 1800s with little support—or even interest—from the evangelical community. These laws remained in place, with few changes, until the second part of the twentieth century.

During the 1960s, many were beginning to feel the laws—which ostensibly prohibited abortions unless the mother's life was at risk—were too restrictive. The American Law Institute recommended allowing abortions to protect the mother's health, broadly defined. In the late 1960s, feminist organizations, together with the American Medical Association, also rallied behind more lenient legislation. Thus, many states began repealing their abortion laws.

Although evangelical Christians were not involved in helping pass America's first antiabortion laws, they were involved in helping overturn them. In contrast to Roman Catholics (and some liberal Protestants), who generally remained opposed to abortion from conception onward, evangelical symposia and publications questioned both the "life begins at conception" stance of Catholics and also, the rigidity of prevailing anti-abortion policies. A leading professor of Old Testament from the famously conservative Dallas Theological Seminary (Bruce Waltke) countered the Roman Catholic position as non-biblical, drawing on the familiar Exodus 21 passage. In a special 1968 issue of *Christianity Today* on contraception and abortion, he wrote in the leading article:

> God does not regard the fetus as a soul, no matter how
> far gestation has progressed. The Law plainly exacts:
> "If a man kills any human life he will be put to death"
> (Lev. 24:17). But according to Exodus 21:22–24, the
> destruction of the fetus is not a capital offense. . . .
> Clearly, then, in contrast to the mother, the fetus is not
> reckoned as a soul.

Another professor from Dallas Theological Seminary—Norman Geisler—argued for the permissibility of abortion in a 1971 book, stating "The embryo is not fully human—it is an undeveloped person." Articles in the evangelical *Christian Life* also drew on Exodus 21: "The Bible definitely pinpoints a difference in the value of a fetus and an adult. Thus, the Bible would appear to disagree with the official Catholic view that the tiniest fetus is as important as an adult human being." One professor of theology, writing in *Christianity Today*, urged a spirit of humility on any who would counter abortion: "We . . . must reckon with the fact that there are those within the Christian community who can see no final offense in abortion when entered into responsibly by a woman in consultation with a physician."

A number of resolutions also flowed from major evangelical organizations. In 1971, for example, the Southern Baptist Convention urged more lenient abortion laws in a formal resolution: "We call upon Southern Baptists to work for legislation that will allow the possibility of abortion under such conditions as rape, incest, clear evidence of severe fetal deformity, and carefully ascertained evidence of the likelihood of damage to the emotional, mental, and physical health of the mother" (a position the convention reiterated after *Roe v. Wade,* in 1974 and 1976).

Perhaps the most significant call for repeal was made by a 1968 gathering hosted by *Christianity Today* and the Christian Medical Society. Evangelical scholars, pastors, and physicians gathered from around the country to produce "A Protestant Affirmation on the Control of Human Reproduction," the stated consensus of those at the symposium. The document affirmed, "The scholars at the convention represent the conservative or evangelical position within Protestantism. . . . [T]hey shared a common acceptance of the Bible as the final authority on moral issues." In addition to reaffirming the view that "procreation . . . is not the sole purpose of the sexual relationship," the signatories also provided Christians with moral guidance on abortion. "The Christian physician will advise induced abortion only to safeguard greater values sanctioned by Scripture," the document notes. "These values should include individual health, family welfare, and social responsibility. . . . When principles conflict, the preservation of fetal life . . . may have to be abandoned in order to maintain full and secure family life." The document sums up the consensus of attendees thus: "Whether or not the performance of an induced abortion is sinful we are not agreed, but about the necessity of it and permissibility for it under certain circumstances we are in accord." These pro-abortion sentiments waned only slightly following *Roe v. Wade* (1973) before being obliterated in the popular evangelical community in the 1980s, with the rise of the evangelical Right.

The Rise of the Evangelical Right (1975–1979)

Traditional wisdom has it that *Roe v. Wade* (1973) was such a shock to the evangelical community that it immediately mobilized en masse to defend "the unborn." In reality, the evangelical response to *Roe* was decidedly ambivalent. A few evangelical leaders were uncomfortable with the ruling—some felt it evinced anti-Christian bias, others supported some abortions but felt *Roe* went too far, and still others never felt comfortable about abortion in the first place—and their views were published in Christian periodicals. In 1975, a few evangelicals came together to "determine a proper Biblical response to abortion-on-demand," resulting in the Christian Action Council (CAC). But neither change had much influence on the broader evangelical culture. As one founder of the CAC noted, "We really thought it wouldn't take much to get the general Christian community in the United States really upset about this issue because it seemed so horrible to us. We thought, 'Once people realize what's going on, there will be a spontaneous upheaval.' That didn't happen." Indeed, Jerry Falwell did not preach a sermon on abortion until 1978. A former president of the Southern Baptist Convention came out in support of *Roe* ("What is best for the mother and for the future should be allowed"), and the *Baptist Press* declared that "religious liberty, human equality and justice are advanced by the Supreme Court abortion decision."

Although evangelicalism featured a wide range of opinions after *Roe*, Roman Catholicism did not. With official teaching from the pope that life is to be treated as an ensouled person "from the moment of conception," Catholics immediately formed the National Right to Life Committee after *Roe* and became politically involved, calling abortion at any stage the murder of unborn babies. Thus, as late as 1980 the evangelical *Moody Monthly*—by now committed to an antiabortion agenda—was still complaining about lack of concern in the broader evangelical community: "Evangelicalism as a whole has uttered no real outcry. We've organized no protest. Do we need more time to think abortion through? . . . The Catholics have called abortion 'The Silent Holocaust.' The deeper horror is the silence of the evangelical."

Despite these initial efforts, the socially conservative political movement that has come to be known as the evangelical Right was not born out of concern about abortion. Randall Balmer, a professor of American religious history at Columbia University and editor at large for *Christianity Today*, has argued convincingly that a bigger motivation for the founding of the evangelical Right was the government's censure of evangelical schools engaged in racial discrimination. Political scientist Duane Oldfield explains: "The most far-reaching federal intervention in local affairs during the 1960s and 1970s was its effort on behalf of desegregation. . . . The civil rights revolution was a challenge to the beliefs of many evangelicals. Even among those who did not directly oppose it, the federal government's aggressive intervention in local affairs served to unsettle habitual subcultural patterns." Evangelicals had remained largely isolated from the broader culture since the Scopes trial in 1925 and had not significantly rethought their assumptions and practices surrounding race. Thus, they took the government's attempts at promoting integration as a hostile intrusion. The evangelical Right formed to respond.

This analysis isn't merely an outsider's perspective. As Balmer notes, it is confirmed by those within the movement. As Paul Weyrich, one of the founders of the evangelical Right, affirms:

> [W]hat galvanized the Christian community was not abortion, school prayer, or the ERA [Equal Rights Amendment]. I am living witness to that because I was trying to get those people interested in those issues and I utterly failed. What changed their minds was Jimmy Carter's intervention against the Christian schools, trying to deny them tax-exempt status on the basis of so-called de facto segregation.

Weyrich's story is confirmed by Ed Dobson, cofounder of Jerry Falwell's Moral Majority activist group: "The Religious New Right did not start because of a concern about abortion. . . . I sat in the non-smoke-filled back room with the Moral Majority, and I frankly do not remember abortion ever being mentioned as a reason why we ought to do something."

"Government interference in Christian schools" roused evangelicals to action, Dobson notes. The evangelical Right, therefore, was not as concerned about abortion initially as it was with defending racially segregated schools. Abortion was picked up later, after evangelicals had been mobilized toward that end.

The irony of this history, Balmer points out, is that contemporary leaders of the evangelical Right are fond of comparing their antiabortion advocacy to the work of the evangelicals who fought slavery in the 1800s. Chuck Colson frequently likens himself to William Wilberforce; Ralph Reed held up Martin Luther King Jr. as inspiration for his Christian Coalition's political activism; many in the movement sing "We Shall Over-come" at pro-life rallies. Yet the lowly origins of the evangelical Right belie all such claims to moral authority. As Balmer notes: "Whereas evangelical abolitionists of the nineteenth century sought freedom for African Americans, the Religious Right of the late twentieth century organized to perpetuate racial discrimination."

It was only after evangelicals got involved in politics to defend seg-regated schools that the contemporary agenda of the evangelical Right began to take form. As they emerged from isolation into cultural par-ticipation, evangelicals—committed to social norms from an idealized past—were disturbed by other changes afoot in American culture. Sev-eral evangelical organizations formed in the late 1970s, opposing the Equal Rights Amendment, feminism, homosexuality, and advocating the return of mandatory school prayer.

How did the evangelical Right come to embrace an antiabortion platform? One of the biggest influences on the developing movement was a man by the name of Francis Schaeffer. Schaeffer, who held a master's degree from Westminster Theological Seminary, had for some time been speaking out against "secular humanism," a new ideology—characterized by a rejection of the supernatural in science and morality—associated in the popular evangelical press with a host of evils, including, in the words of one evangelical magazine, "women's liberation," "the ERA" [Equal Rights Amendment], "evolution," "sex education," "the loss of patriotism," and "many of the other problems that are tearing America apart today." Later in his career, Schaeffer would argue that Christians should use civil disobedience and, if necessary, force, to install young earth creationism in public schools. In his book and video series *How Should We Then Live?*, Schaeffer acquainted evangelicals with secular humanism. His main min-istry began in Champéry, Switzerland, although he was kicked out of the city in 1954 because of his attempts to evangelize Roman Catholics.

Schaeffer argued that America was founded on Judeo-Christian values and that Christians should fight to return their government to those values. He was the prime force in goading Jerry Falwell into political activism. Initially, Falwell was skeptical of politics; he was well aware that the fundamentalists and evangelicals he associated with did not constitute a large enough force to alter the course of government. But Schaeffer would have none of it: "Listen, God used pagans to do his work in the Old Testament, so why don't you use pagans to do your work now?" Thus, the evangelical Right eventually learned to increase its power by cooperating with Roman Catholics, Mormons, mainline Protestants, and other "pagans" who shared similar, socially conservative political goals.

Schaeffer—who saw abortion as a symptom of decline in respect for human life in the broader culture—was responsible for making opposition to abortion a staple of the evangelical Right's political platform. In 1979, he cooperated with the surgeon C. Everett Koop to produce a book and film series on abortion titled *Whatever Happened to the Human Race?* The film series was probably the single most important factor in convincing the evangelical Right to oppose abortion. The central argument of the book is that at one time, most people in America adhered to a "Judeo-Christian consensus" that human life was special, and therefore, should be treated with the utmost respect. As a result of the widespread acceptance of evolution and naturalism, both of which Schaeffer perceived as lowering the status of humans to animals or machines, this sense gradually eroded to the rock bottom level it reached when *Roe v.Wade* was passed. Unless Christians mobilized to stop abortion, the authors argued that infanticide and involuntary euthanasia would soon be widespread. Interestingly, given the rhetoric of the contemporary pro-life movement, the book does not argue based on a list of proof-texts and does not rally around the idea that life begins at conception and abortion is murder. These claims would not characterize the evangelical pro-life movement until the early 1980s.

Whatever Happened to the Human Race? was somewhat of an affront to evangelical scholars at the time. In the midst of widespread disagreement among evangelicals over abortion, Schaeffer and Koop decided to forgo the long, hard process of convincing their academic opponents to accept their position on abortion, and instead, after writing the book, hit the road to present their film to popular audiences (on a tour across America) as "the Biblical view." Schaeffer, who went by "Dr. Schaeffer" despite his lack of an earned doctorate, presents himself in the introduction as "one of the world's most respected thinkers." No mention was made that a significant portion of evangelicals did not adhere to his view.

The book spent less than one paragraph on Christian history, where the authors cite the views of early Christian theologian Tertullian, who believed life begins at conception because the soul is transmitted with semen, as representative of the entire Christian tradition (in fact, his views were condemned as heresy by Aquinas and several church fathers and popes), and less than three paragraphs discuss directly relevant biblical passages. The central argument of the book and film was not in fact uniquely Christian at all, but simply one big, dramatic slippery slope argument. For Schaeffer and Koop, abortion degraded and commodified all human life by giving some humans say over the lives of others. Indeed, we are warned in the preface that legalized abortion inevitably "will lead to death for all but the planned and perfect members of our society." The film featured booming horror-movie music, with images of screaming toddlers locked up in cages, hundreds of plastic babies strewn across the shore of the Dead Sea, plastic babies moving down a conveyor belt where a quality control inspector violently eliminated those with defects, and an ominous narrator in the background, promising audiences that if they didn't mobilize to stop abortion, very soon, the government would start killing even adult humans who simply were not intelligent enough. One scene in the film features a couple at the grocery store where, in addition to other supplies, they also pick up a living child and casually place him in their shopping cart.

What is remarkable about the film is its portrait of *Roe v. Wade* as the sordid conclusion to a long, steady decline from the morally pristine time of the founding fathers. Indeed, for all their grand historical claims about "the Judeo-Christian consensus" that supposedly once ruled early America, they fail to mention that abortion was legal in America during the time period they were idealizing—and that it was legal, in large part, *because* of Christian beliefs. And the fact Schaeffer and Koop would choose the 1970s as the absolute rock-bottom point in terms of respect for life only reveals their narrow scope. Looking back on history from an African American perspective, for example, one would recall several hundred years of brutal enslavement, followed by freedom from slavery after the Civil War in the 1800s, followed by several decades of severe economic oppression and racism, followed by a long, hard-fought campaign to end segregation that climaxed in the 1970s with the success of the civil rights movement (a campaign from which both of the white males now concerned about "human life" were absent). The 1970s also featured widespread opposition to war in the wake of Vietnam, a Supreme Court ban on capital punishment, a movement to make buildings more accessible for the handicapped, and the emergence of feminism as a force for women's equality.

Nevertheless, the scare strategy worked and it worked well. The broader evangelical world was shaken by the video's images and threats of inevitable descent into mandatory killing, and the emerging evangelical Right organizations added abortion to their list of America's sins. Schaeffer's views were widely disseminated in the evangelical community, providing the ideology of the burgeoning evangelical Right, and eagerly embraced by would-be culture warriors. Among them were Pat Robertson, Jerry Falwell, James Dobson, and Chuck Colson, who were celebrating Francis Schaeffer's work by the 1980s and doing their best with newly formed Religious Right organizations to reclaim the "Judeo-Christian nation" he described.

As evangelicals emerged from isolation to political participation in

the late 1970s, a variety of forces also emerged to regulate their perceptions and beliefs on political issues of the day. As political scientist Jared
Farley notes, "The political mobilization of evangelicals was the result
of a top-down phenomenon, in which evangelical elites formulated and
communicated an ideology of conservative politics and collective action
to their followers." Over the course of the 1970s, *Christianity Today* and
similar evangelical magazines became increasingly politicized and parti-
san, foreshadowing the later politicization of evangelical Christianity as
a whole. In the 1960s, claims like the following were common: "In the
complexities of politics it is often difficult—and sometimes well-nigh
impossible—for anyone to assert that a given viewpoint is the Christian
position." Political diversity within evangelicalism was acceptable, the idea
of one unified "Christian political agenda" simplistic. Such claims were ef-
fectively absent in the 1980s, by which time the periodicals were not coy
about advancing "the Christian position" on a variety of issues. Characteristic was *Christian Life*'s praise of the Religious Right in 1980 for waging
war on common "liberal enemies" (a term now encompassing Democrats,
feminists, homosexuals, supporters of *Roe v. Wade*, and the like).

Religious Right organizations began to play the biggest role in the
politicization of evangelicalism, regulating perceptions of both the world
outside their communities and of "what the Bible says" about particular
issues of the day. Both the Bible and the world at large were interpreted
in mailings, the radio, TV shows, and even model sermons (mailed to
pastors to teach congregants how to "vote their faith") to advance their
antiabortion, antihomosexuality, antifeminism, and antievolution goals.
One group, for example, distributed "Biblical Scorecards" by mass mail
to millions of evangelicals, ranking candidates based on how well their
positions lined up with "the biblical position" on a range of issues. Direct
mailings often warned that if certain "liberal" policies came to pass, the
culture as a whole would descend into immoral chaos. Pat Robertson
characterized the movement for female equality as a "socialist, anti-family

political movement that encourages women to leave their husbands, kill their children, practice witchcraft, destroy capitalism and become lesbians." The Christian Coalition told followers that activists who sought equality for gays and lesbians wanted to use evangelical "tax money to teach their sons how to sodomize each other."

How the Bible Began Saying That Life Begins at Conception (1980 to Present)

Around 1980, what is now widely considered by evangelicals to be "the biblical position on abortion" was invented. To understand why this way of interpreting the Bible arose, it is necessary to recall a bit of the history we have surveyed thus far. In 1869, the Roman Catholic Church accepted the official position that, for all practical purposes, "life begins at conception," a position that had stayed in effect to this day. Since they accepted this position for many reasons evangelicals do not share—including belief that Mary was conceived without sin, Platonic conceptions of human identity, and official statements from the pope—the position had not gained a strong hold in the evangelical community. Thus, while evangelicals generally supported more lax abortion laws in the late 1960s, Catholics vigorously opposed them; while evangelicals did not exhibit much of a reaction following *Roe v. Wade* in 1973, Roman Catholics were outraged.

In 1973, Catholics founded the National Right to Life Committee, with the goal of passing a "human life amendment" that would define the fetus as a person in the US Constitution "from the moment of conception." The National Right to Life Committee quickly became the most powerful antiabortion organization in American politics. In 1974, the Catholic Church established as official doctrine that the fetus has a "Right to Life." While evangelicals were lying in an apolitical, pre–Religious Right slumber, Catholics were establishing what might be called the "ideology" of the antiabortion movement, the vocabulary and concepts that would frame the issue of abortion in the public square: that the fetus is an "innocent," "unborn baby" with a "Right to Life" "from the moment of conception." By the time Koop and Schaeffer took their tour across America in 1979, Catholics had established what it meant to be "pro-life" in the political world. Although Koop and Schaeffer aroused antiabortion sentiments among evangelicals and placed the issue within a decline-of-civilization narrative that resonated with the community, they were not the origin of what are perhaps the evangelical antiabortion movement's most significant features: claims that the Bible says "life begins at conception" and claims about the "Right to Life" of the fetus (both of which entail that abortion is murder, and thus, have tremendous political consequences). The "life begins at conception" and "Right to Life" rhetoric arose from political cooperation with Catholics.

As evangelicals embraced the antiabortion stance full throttle around 1980, they joined arms with well-funded and well-organized Catholic organizations, such as the National Right to Life Committee, that had been working on the issue for nearly a decade. In the face of an evangelical scholarly community divided on how to think about fetal life, the evangelical Right no doubt appreciated the stark and uncompromising stance their allies had developed. It is much easier, in a political world hostile to fine distinctions and nuance, to declare that abortion at any stage of pregnancy is murder—period. Several evangelical Right leaders also believed that Catholics would be drawn to an uncompromising antiabortion position, expanding their political base. Therefore, leaders of evangelical Right organizations began appropriating the vocabulary and concepts of Catholic pro-life organizations and using them in mass mailers, radio broadcasts, and television shows: that the fetus is an "innocent" "unborn baby" with a "Right to Life" "from the moment of conception." Indeed, one of the evangelical Right's first political moves against abortion was to join Catholics in sponsoring the "Human Life Statute" in 1981, which would define the fetus as a person in the US Constitution "from the moment of conception" (they cooperated extensively on other occasions as well).

Although Catholics had articulated their views on fetal life for many uniquely Catholic reasons noted previously, and thus never felt any need to suggest their position was "the biblical view," for evangelicals who claim to live by scripture alone, this strategy would never work. But this wasn't an insurmountable problem; like all texts, the Bible is malleable and can be made to say just about anything to suit the political interests of its interpreters, with a de-emphasis on some verses here (in this case, Exodus 21) and an emphasis on others there (in this case, Psalm 139 and Luke 1, interpreted with the fundamentalist proclivity for finding precise factual information in the Bible's narratives and poetry). Thus, when they emerged as a new antiabortion force around 1980, the leaders of the evangelical Right simply began reinterpreting the Bible so as to legitimate the ideology of Roman Catholic pro-life organizations and therefore recruit "Bible only" evangelicals into their Catholic/Evangelical coalition.

One of the first instances of this phenomenon was in Jerry Falwell's *Listen, America!* (1980), which featured his first sustained discussion of abortion—in a chapter titled, significantly, "The Right to Life." "The Bible clearly states that life begins at conception," he declares, referencing Luke 1:39–44 and Psalm 139:13–16. "Abortion is not birth control nor family planning. It is murder according to the Word of God. . . . Last year more than 1.5 million little babies were murdered in America. . . . It is time that medical students as well as every other person in our United States put those words 'from the time of conception' back into their thinking." Falwell made sure his followers did just that by disseminating his biblical interpretations to millions of evangelicals across America. One of his direct mailers, titled "Scriptures for Life," featured a set of Bible verses that demonstrated what God's position was on abortion: God viewed all abortions as murder from the moment of conception onward. Focus on the

Family employed a similar strategy, claiming to provide in its literature "Scripture verses that speak to the value of preborn life created in God's image from the moment of fertilization." Other pro-life organizations used quotes from the Bible in bumper stickers and newsletters, giving the impression that they were simply appropriating "the biblical position" on the matter. According to one widely distributed discussion of the Bible, Exodus 21 commanded the execution of all abortionists.

By the mid-1980s, the evangelical Right was so successful with this strategy that the popular evangelical community would no longer tolerate any alternative position. Hence, the outrage over a book titled *Brave New People* published by InterVarsity Press in 1984. In addition to discussing a number of new biotechnologies, including genetic engineering and in vitro fertilization, the author, an evangelical professor living in New Zealand, also devoted a chapter to abortion. His position was similar to that of most evangelicals fifteen years prior. Although he did not believe the fetus was a full-fledged person from conception, he did believe that because it was a potential person, it should be treated with respect. Abortion was only permissible to protect the health and well-being of the mother, to preclude a severely deformed child, and in a few other hard cases, such as rape and incest.

Although this would have been an unremarkable book in 1970, the popular evangelical community was outraged. Evangelical magazines and popular leaders across the country decried the book and its author, and evangelicals picketed outside the publisher's office and urged booksellers to boycott the publisher. One writer called it a "monstrous book." Another stated the book could only be produced by those who have "accommodated themselves to the world," who are "on a bandwagon bound for hell." Francis Schaeffer's son called it "a noxious dish of reviving the eugenics movement of death as a solution to social problems." He also stated the Christian publisher should shut down. Evangelical laypeople decried the book in letters to the editor at magazines like *Christianity*

Today. The popular response to the book—despite its endorsements from Carl F. H. Henry, the first editor of *Christianity Today*, and Lew Smedes, an evangelical professor of ethics at Fuller Theological Seminary—was so overwhelmingly hostile that the book became the first ever withdrawn by InterVarsity Press over the course of nearly half a century in business.

The book was republished a year later by Eerdmans Press. In a preface, the author noted, "The heresy of which I appear to be guilty is that I cannot state categorically that human/personal life commences at day one of gestation. This, it seems, is being made a basic affirmation of evangelicalism, from which there can be no deviation. . . . No longer is it sufficient to hold classic evangelical affirmations on the nature of biblical revelation, the person and work of Christ, or justification by faith alone. In order to be labeled an evangelical, it is now essential to hold a particular view of the status of the embryo and fetus."

Later in the 1980s, the "life begins at conception" position was so widely taken for granted that even some scholars—generally, those at fundamentalist Bible schools, colleges, and seminaries, ranging from Jerry Falwell's Liberty University to Portland's Multnomah Bible College— were now advocating it. A case in point is a book published by Multnomah Press in 1987 by Paul Fowler, a professor at a small Bible school in the South. "The Bible shows life begins at conception," he states. "Scripture places a high importance on conception," he argues, because it uses the word "conception" several times. "In the Genesis narratives alone, the phrase 'conceived and bore' is found eleven times. The close pairing of the two words clearly emphasizes conception, not birth, as the starting point of life." He concludes from James 1:15 ("when lust has conceived, it gives birth to sin") that it is "obvious" that James considers "conception the beginning of the matter." He asks: "Does not the attempt to undervalue the importance of conception for the beginning of human life go contrary to the clear teaching of Scripture?" In a concluding section titled "Scripture Is Clear!" he states that the Bible "provides a thorough and clear response to abortion." He asks, "When does life begin?" He answers, "At conception."

Although "life begins at conception" and "baby-murder" rhetoric is now widely embraced by leaders of the evangelical Right, assumed to be "the biblical position on abortion" by nearly all lay evangelicals, and also advocated at a number of Bible colleges and fundamentalist seminaries, it seems a large number of evangelical scholars were never convinced. A host of evangelical professors opposed the popular culture's position, many arguing that evangelicals should not be attempting to change abortion laws. This includes Lewis Smedes (1983: "Abortion should be legally permitted during the first six weeks of pregnancy"); Carl F. H. Henry of *Christianity Today* (1984: "The scriptural correlation of sexual intercourse with marriage . . . implies an ethical basis for voluntary abortion in cases of incest and rape"); Robert N. Wennberg of Westmont College (1985: "Abortion is not murder . . . abortion ought not to be criminalized"); Allen Verhey of Hope College, Edward Langerak of St. Olaf College, Douglas Diekma of Edgewood College, and Hessel Bouma III and Theodore Rottman of Calvin College (all of whom wrote in 1989: "We should not support a right-to-life amendment that would grant personhood to fetuses from conception . . . personhood should be morally and legally granted to the fetus at the end of the second trimester"); and James C. Peterson of McMaster Divinity College (2003: "When precisely [embryos] become persons is not taught in these texts," referring to oft-cited biblical passages), among others.

Like the author of *Brave New People*, these scholars were largely ignored or demonized by the popular evangelical community. After Calvin College professor Hessel Bouma published his book on abortion, for example, the president of Calvin received a steady stream of letters, demanding Bouma be fired for holding his views. Wheaton College resisted attempts by students in 1984 to put forth an official college position on the full moral status of human life "from the moment of conception" since a large block of its faculty did not agree with the popular evangelical culture's position. Even C. Everett Koop, coauthor of *Whatever Happened to the Human Race?*, distanced himself from the pro-life movement in the late 1980s, turned off by its militant stance: "[T]hey had an all-or-nothing mentality. They wanted it all, and they got nothing."

Although they got nothing from the broader culture, by the end of the 1980s, leaders of the evangelical Right had achieved much within the evangelical community. "God's position on abortion" was gradually modified in the popular evangelical community in the late 1970s, shifting from the 1960s declaration that "God does not regard the fetus as a soul no matter how far gestation has progressed" to the early 1980s position that "the Bible clearly states that life begins at conception," the long history of biblical interpretation to the contrary notwithstanding. In the process, God's position became, right down the line—from the moment of conception, one might say—almost exactly the same as the position of the evangelical Right's more established and politically powerful Catholic allies, most notably, the National Right to Life Committee. The concomitant shift in the interpretation of the Bible was not occasioned by new discoveries about the ancient meaning of the text or new scientific developments; it was occasioned by a shift in the historical context and political interests of evangelical leaders.

Millions of evangelicals—who have been socialized by mass mailings, radio programs, and Christian magazines to interpret the Bible as teaching that life begins at conception—think they are merely "submitting to the authority of God's Word" by voting single-mindedly for candidates who support criminalizing abortion, elevating abortion above every other political issue, opposing human embryonic stem cell research, and otherwise acting in accordance with this interpretation of the Bible. In fact, they are submitting to the sublimated political interests of other humans.

Science and Reason

The evangelical antiabortion movement is not driven solely by biblical interpretations, however. Over the years, several arguments from science and reason have been marshaled to support the cause. One of the most common scientific arguments is that there has been a discovery since the time of past theologians that proves fetal personhood begins at conception.

What discovery might that be? Those making this argument usually don't say. Some say scientists now know human life exists at conception. While this is true from a biological perspective—like every cell in the human body, the embryo is indeed living and human—it isn't a new discovery, nor does it have any necessary moral implications. Thomas Aquinas, for example, who argued that full moral life did not begin until the brain developed, believed the embryo had a life initially resembling that of a plant (implantation and growth in the uterus), then an animal (presence of rudimentary organs), then a person (sentient intellectual life with the development of the brain). And even if we ignore past Christian theology on this front, it is not true biologically that human life begins at conception, even if it is present then. The cells composing the embryo come from previous cells, which are also living and biologically human.

Of course, the embryo is unique because, unlike the sperm and egg, it can develop into a person; therefore, according to some thinkers, it is a person. But if the embryo can become a person, so can each of the cells composing it. This is how identical twins and triplets form; some cells break off from the early embryo and continue developing. If having the capacity to develop into a person is sufficient to make an entity a person, then multiple people compose the early embryo. Furthermore, with advanced cloning technology, each of the nuclei in the some seventy-five trillion cells of the human body could potentially drive the development of a human person. Although the potential to become a person may warrant significant respect—perhaps enough that embryos shouldn't be deliberately created and destroyed for research purposes—being able to become a person does not make one a person, any more than being an acorn makes one an oak tree.

Others say that science shows us a clear dividing line in the process of development: conception. In the blink of an eye, a sperm and egg merge to form an embryo. Science, according to the proponents of this argument, proves that life begins at the moment of conception. But conception is not actually a moment; it is a process lasting several days, involving many shorter processes. These include the process of the egg and the sperm that will fertilize it entering the fallopian tube, the sperm membrane contacting and then binding the egg membrane, the fusing of sperm and egg membranes, the sperm nucleus entering the egg cytoplasm (which at this point contains two nuclei and three sets of chromosomes), the process of meiosis II (during which the egg nucleus divides and expels a set of chromosomes), the process of the egg nucleus fusing with the sperm nucleus, and the processes of the embryo dividing and then implanting in the womb, among others. At which point during these processes does the "the moment of conception" occur? When can we say that before this point we simply have cells but afterward we have a person, morally equivalent to you or me? Yes, one can point to a part of this process and decide to treat what comes after it as a person. But the process itself does not tell one where to point. Science may illuminate human development, but it can't answer the metaphysical question of when personhood begins.

Although science does not prove full moral life begins at conception, it does provide a significant difficulty for that conclusion. Due to hormone imbalances, genetic anomalies, and a number of unknown factors, between 50 percent and 75 percent of embryos fail to implant in the uterus and are passed with the monthly menstrual flow. If we agree with pro-life advocates that every embryo is as morally valuable as an adult human, this means more than half of humans immediately die. This fact provides pro-life advocates with an opportunity to follow through on their convictions. Surely, a moral response to a pandemic of this magnitude would be to rally the scientific community to devote the vast majority of its efforts to better understanding why this happens and trying to stop it. Yet the same pro-life leaders who declare that every embryo is morally equivalent to a fully developed child have done nothing to advocate such research. Granted, many of these embryos have severe enough chromosomal anomalies that one could argue they are not even humans or could not possibly be saved if they were. But even if medicine could save only 10 percent of these embryos—and we don't know because no one has cared enough to ask—it would be saving more lives than curing HIV, diabetes, and malaria combined. One could say that this massive loss of human life is natural, and therefore, humans are under no obligation to end it. But it is not clear why the same argument could not be used to justify complacency in the face of AIDS, cancer, heart disease, and other natural causes of human death.

If arguments from science fail to prove that life begins at conception, what about arguments from reason? Probably the most popular pro-life argument on this front is to hold up enormous pictures of aborted fetuses in public or to show videos of abortions using an ultrasound. These pictures are then taken to establish a whole list of moral conclusions about abortion, which only a deranged or morally callous person could deny.

One problem with this approach is that the same argument can just as easily be used by pro-choice advocates, who hold up placards of bloated, dead women with blood-soaked vaginas—victims of the type of illegal abortions practiced prior to *Roe*—as self-evidently establishing that abortion should be legal and safe. One might also hold up pictures of soldiers torn apart by war as self-evidently establishing that war is never justified. One could probably even make a case for outlawing brain surgery this way, holding up disgusting pictures of bodies with their head split open during an operation. The trick is to get observers to transmute the intensity of their disgust at grotesque pictures into an intense level of confidence that whatever enabled these pictures must always be wrong. It works on some people, but that doesn't make it a valid moral argument.

Like the position that full moral life begins at conception, the position implied by gruesome posters of aborted fetuses—that abortion is mass murder—has implications no mainstream pro-life organization accepts. To see why, one needs only to consider the antiabortion violence that has occurred over the past thirty years. Ever since the evangelical Right began disseminating the Roman Catholic position to evangelicals as the biblical view, many have decided that simply voting for pro-life candidates during election season is not sufficient. These individuals have set fire to and bombed abortion clinics, sent hate mail and made harassing calls to both abortion doctors and women procuring their services, and blockaded the doors of abortion clinics. Other pro-life activists have taken up arms and killed abortion doctors.

All such acts of violence are swiftly condemned by mainstream pro-life organizations. A 1991 article in *Christianity Today*, titled "You Say Choice, I Say Murder," condemned 1984 clinic bombings sponsored by the Gideon Project. Pro-life groups immediately condemned the 1994 murder of two abortion clinic receptionists in Massachusetts. When abortion provider George Tiller was murdered in 2009, representatives of pro-life organizations quickly took to the airwaves to condemn the act (not neglecting, of course, to condemn the "holocaust of abortion" in the same breath).

And here we find the rub for mainstream pro-life groups, particularly those in the evangelical community. Because most of the leaders associated with the evangelical Right are not pacifists—as we saw earlier, evangelicals were the most likely religious group in America to support the Iraq war—it makes little sense for them to simultaneously hold that abortion is on par morally with the organized slaughter of children *and* that Christians may not use violence to end it. Many leaders of the Religious Right supported the war in Iraq and the execution of Saddam Hussein, reasoning that because this leader was killing other people, it was morally permissible to invade Iraq and kill him. Dietrich Bonhoeffer, one of the celebrated Protestant theologians of the twentieth century, plotted with several other Christians in Nazi Germany to assassinate Hitler. Because Hitler was presiding over genocide, they took it as their moral duty to take up arms and end his life. Other heroes of the Holocaust are the Jews who killed Nazi soldiers presiding over the gas chambers. Imagine the Holocaust spread to America and millions of children were being rounded up and killed. Would we praise Christians who proposed to settle the matter simply by voting for "antigenocide" candidates during election season—even if that strategy had failed to end the Holocaust after forty years?

If there was ever a legitimate occasion for nonpacifists to use violence in defense of justice, surely it would be during a forty-year campaign of state-sponsored genocide directed against innocent humans who are unable to defend themselves. This is especially true in the case of abortion, where in the United States alone, the death toll would be almost ten times higher than that of the Jews killed in the Holocaust (fifty million versus six million). If pro-life evangelical leaders truly believe abortion is mass murder, one might reasonably ask why they are not encouraging their followers to take up the mantle of Bonhoeffer and use whatever means are necessary, including violence, to end it. That they not only refrain from doing so, but also strongly condemn such actions, suggests that all the talk of unborn children, the Holocaust, and baby genocide serves little other purpose than stirring up passions and votes.

Abortion and Single-Issue Politics

The campaign to criminalize abortion has dominated evangelical politics for the past thirty years. In the minds of many, perhaps most, lay

evangelicals, who constitute roughly 35 percent of the American population, it doesn't ultimately matter what a politician is doing to combat
economic oppression, help marginalized groups, promote world peace,
or even promote US interests. These issues may impact the enthusiasm
evangelicals have for a given politician, but they seldom determine the
direction evangelicals vote (the small community of left-wing evangelicals notwithstanding). At the end of the day, all that really matters is that
a politician identifies as "pro-life."

And quite logically. For a community that thinks embryos are morally equivalent to fully developed humans, abortion becomes genocide
on an unprecedented scale. "Expanding the issue agenda" becomes morally indefensible. Settling for abortion reduction becomes settling for
legalized murder. Allowing abortion in so-called hard cases—for raped
women, or pregnancies resulting from incest—is equivalent to allowing
the murder of one person to improve the lot of another. Uncompromising single-issue politics flows naturally from the belief that life begins at
conception and abortion is murder.

It is unfortunate, then, that a position with such tremendous political, social, and moral implications—held with such intense conviction
in the evangelical community—rests on such a flimsy foundation. It can
claim biblical support only through tendentious and historically recent
interpretations; it contradicts the dominant tradition of Christian thought
on when moral life begins; it is not required by new scientific discoveries;
and even those who adhere to it fail to take it to its logical conclusions.
For the past thirty years, evangelicals have spent nearly all their political
energy on behalf of a position they have little basis to accept.

Evangelicals can and should expand the issue agenda to include concern about poverty, environmentalism, public schools, and global peace.
And they should compromise, open crisis pregnancy centers, and work
to alleviate social and economic circumstances that cause women to
seek abortions in the first place. Abandoning the belief that abortion is

mass murder does not require concluding that it's okay after all. It may still be morally wrong and bad for society, even if not as bad as previously believed. But any embrace of mediating positions on abortion, and any broadening of the evangelical political agenda, will only be intelligible after evangelicals reject the belief that abortion kills babies from conception onward.

THREE

Queer Quagmires:

Evolution, Higher Criticism, and Homosexuality

ON AUGUST 19, 2009, a tornado formed just outside Minneapolis. The mass of dirt and wind weaved its way downtown, splitting trees, toppling power lines, and damaging houses along the way. It blew through a record store and middle school and knocked over the steeple of a downtown Lutheran church. It left seven thousand people temporarily without power, but no deaths or serious injuries occurred. A cleanup crew quickly took to the streets, and the Minneapolis police circled neighborhoods to check on residents. The incident most likely would have been written off as a random occurrence, unfortunate but not devastating—except for the fact that the Evangelical Lutheran Church of America (ECLA) was holding its national convention that day. On the list of topics for discussion was the moral status of same-sex relationships. A vote was to follow the discussion, though the tornado delayed both till later in the day. But the ECLA ultimately voted to welcome those in gay relationships into the communion and ministry of the church.

For one local onlooker, the combination of public Christian support for homosexuality and a tornado on the same day, in the same city, could not have been mere coincidence. John Piper, pastor of Bethlehem Baptist Church in Minneapolis, whose influence is so wide he is often thought of as a kind of pope of evangelical Christianity, declared, "The tornado in Minneapolis was a gentle but firm warning to the ECLA and all of us: Turn from the approval of sin. Turn from the promotion of behaviors that lead to destruction. Reaffirm the great Lutheran heritage of allegiance to the truth and authority of Scripture." Piper's declaration was scattered with biblical references intending to demonstrate the sinfulness of homosexuality—and to suggest the tornado was sent by God to punish the ECLA.

In 1999, Christina Van Dyke, currently a tenured professor of philosophy at Calvin College, applied for a job at Wheaton College, widely considered to be the flagship evangelical college. One telling of the story is worth quoting at length: "Van Dyke signed the Statement of Faith and the Community Covenant (Wheaton's code of conduct), but inserted a clarification saying that 'it isn't clear to me that the Bible unambiguously condemns monogamous same-sex relationships.' That did not entail, Van Dyke notes, 'either that I was in favor of them, or that I thought God was.' Rather, it was meant as a hermeneutical point about the precise content of Scripture. The department chair asked Van Dyke whether she would be willing to remove the clarification, since Christianity and homosexuality is the provost's area of expertise and her reservation was 'certain to raise red flags.' But Van Dyke opted to keep the reservation as it was. Sure enough:

> I got a call from Stan Jones [the provost of Wheaton College], asking me a number of questions about my reservations. I kept saying that I was not claiming to have figured this out, but that it was not at all clear to me from my own research and study that the Bible's position on homosexual behavior was unambiguous. We talked about how I would handle students who came to me to talk about questioning their own sexuality, and I said I would be willing to send them elsewhere. He sent me a whole stack of reading

material (much of which he'd written) arguing that the
Bible's position on homosexual behavior was, in fact,
clear. I read it all. . . . It didn't change my mind.

In the end, despite the fact that Van Dyke had a BA from a Christian college, an Ivy League PhD, and the strong support of a Wheaton
department—in addition to being a believer who had signed all of the
relevant statements—her clarification meant that," in Van Dyke's words,
"at about 5 p.m. the day before my interview was scheduled, [the chair]
called in tears to tell me that he'd just finished talking to the provost, and
that I was no longer a candidate for their position."

The cases of John Piper and Wheaton College illustrate two things.
First, unwillingness to consider alternative views on homosexuality is not
merely a property of the extreme Right. It is part of the mainstream
evangelical culture, evinced by its most esteemed scholars and educational institutions. Second, the opponents of homosexuality are losing a
culture war—both in secular America and in Christianity at large. Not
only is America racing toward the legalization of same-sex marriage, but
mainline Christian denominations such as the ECLA, and many younger
evangelicals such as Van Dyke, are questioning past condemnations of gay
marriage. As polls consistently bear out, younger evangelicals harbor considerably less antipathy toward homosexuality than the older generation.
And when it comes to legalized same-sex marriage, in the broader culture, the general consensus is that it is only a matter of time. Although the
argument from inevitability is invalid—just because the culture is moving
toward supporting gay marriage does not mean it should—change is occurring nonetheless. The question is: How should evangelicals respond to
that change?

For much of the 1990s, the evangelical Right waged war not so much
on gay marriage as on homosexuality itself. Campaigns against gay rights,
and in favor of heterosexual conversion programs, were widespread in

evangelicalism. In 1992, James Dobson worked to pass a referendum that prohibited in the state of Colorado "all legislative, executive, or judicial action at any level of state or local government designed to protect the status of persons based on their 'homosexual, lesbian or bisexual orientation.'" His reasoning seemed simple enough: "Communities do not let prostitutes, pedophiles, voyeurs, adulterers, and those who sexually prefer animals to publicly celebrate their lifestyles, so why should homosexuals get such privileges?" The same year, the National Association for the Research and Therapy of Homosexuality (NARTH) was founded, characterizing homosexuality as a mental disorder and publishing books with such titles as *A Parent's Guide to Preventing Homosexuality*. Against the assertions of mainstream scientists, NARTH, Dobson, and other evangelical leaders insisted that homosexuals are homosexuals either due to relational deficiencies in childhood or willful choice. Either way, they characterized "the homosexual lifestyle" as a life of sickness, promiscuity, depression, and suicide. And if gay people are culpable for being gay, then it made sense to many evangelicals to discriminate against them solely on the basis of their sexual orientation. Although Amendment 2 was struck down by the Supreme Court, that didn't stop the movement from powering ahead. Dobson's next major project, begun in earnest at the end of the decade, attempted to help homosexuals change their sexual orientation. "Focus on the Family is promoting the truth that homosexuality is preventable and treatable," literature declared. "There is freedom from homosexuality."

But by the 2000s, the terms of the debate had shifted. At issue was not so much homosexuality itself but gay marriage. Previously, scientific arguments had focused on the etiology of homosexuality and possibilities of changing it. Conservatives argued that homosexuality was either chosen or caused by negative childhood experiences and that, with proper therapy, gays could become straight. Liberals argued that homosexuality is largely genetic or biological and that attempts to convert gays to straights were damaging to gay people. Now, arguments focused more on gay marriage. Can gays have just as fulfilling marriages as heterosexuals (liberals) or are they inherently promiscuous (conservatives)? Do children raised in gay homes do just as well as those raised in straight homes (liberals) or much worse (conservatives)?

In the political sphere, *Lawrence v. Texas* (2003) made Texas's antisodomy laws unconstitutional, a move that, as Justice Antonin Scalia lamented in his dissenting opinion, paved the way for the legalization of same-sex marriage. George W. Bush's reelection was credited in some circles to the placement of amendments against gay marriage on the ballot in eleven states, which increased evangelical turnout (and all of which passed). By 2008, gay marriage was still in the national spotlight. Although the movement against it had suffered setbacks—Ted Haggard, former president of the National Association of Evangelicals and major opponent of homosexuality, was caught with a gay prostitute—it achieved a major victory with the passage of Proposition 8. The measure defined marriage in California as "between a man and a woman" and claimed in its campaign literature that if gay activists got their way, the next step would be to "legalize having sex with children" (at the time of writing Proposition 8 has been struck down as unconstitutional in a US district court). It was enthusiastically endorsed by Rick Warren, James Dobson, and Charles Colson, among other evangelicals, who claimed as their chief motivation a desire to defend the biblical view of marriage.

And indeed, when it comes to homosexuality, there is not only a widespread belief in the evangelical culture that same-sex relations are wrong but also a widespread belief, particularly in the older generation, that this is so unambiguously taught in the Bible that those who disagree— or even are not quite sure about the matter—are intentionally denying the truth. Evangelicals appeal to passages like Leviticus 18:22 and 20:13, 1 Corinthians 6:9 and 1 Timothy 1:9-10, and especially Romans 1:26-27, all usually from a modern English translation of the Bible, as obviously condemning homosexual activity. D. A. Carson, a professor of New Testament at Trinity Evangelical Divinity School, sums up the evangelical consensus best when he characterizes Christian support for gay marriage as "willful defiance of what God has said." For evangelicals like Carson, supporting gay marriage goes against the core of what it means to be a Christian. Christians are supposed to read the Bible and obey it—not twist it to justify their sin. "I suspect that in our generation," Carson continues, "the homosexuality issue is becoming one of those triggering issues . . . that is forcing upon us some profound reflections on whether we will submit to Scripture or not." The debate about homosexuality matters to many evangelicals because, in their minds at least, defending the exclusion of gays from marriage is ultimately about defending the Bible.

Many liberal Christians, who tend to support gay marriage, also understand the gay debate as being ultimately about what the Bible says. In a book with a title that could summarize the theme of almost all the arguments made about Christianity and homosexuality—liberal and conservative—over the past several decades, pro-gay theologian Daniel Helminiak writes on *What the Bible* Really *Says About Homosexuality.* The Bible really says, in his analysis, that same-sex relations aren't sinful. The relevant passages, at least when read in their historical context, really condemn something else. Liberals tend to emphasize broad themes in scripture about love and justice and God's insistence in Genesis 2:18 that "it is not good for the human to be alone" as supporting the inclusion of gays in marriage. Like the evangelical scholars above, many scholars on the liberal side of the debate believe that, when it comes to homosexuality, conservative scholars are intentionally denying the truth. The debate about homosexuality matters to many liberal Christians because, in their minds at least, defending the inclusion of gays in marriage is ultimately about defending the Bible.

Both parties to the debate about homosexuality contain intelligent, pious, and rigorous scholars. Both parties purport to base their positions on exactly the same book. And both parties come to diametrically opposed conclusions. Many explain this disagreement by postulating that one side of the debate—conservative or liberal—is simply biased. Conservatives are blinded by homophobia. Liberals are blinded by political correctness. If the other guys were truly objective, in this analysis, they would see things the same way we do. And there are many on both sides who embrace this line of thought, explaining disagreement over the Bible by vilifying the other side. But for those who don't find this assessment convincing, there is a better explanation for why Christian scholars disagree: The debate over homosexuality is not about defending the Bible at all.

Interpreting Interpreting

When liberal and conservative Christians expect that a truly careful reading of scripture should produce consensus in the debate on homosexuality, they are adhering to the philosophy of a man by the name of Francis Bacon. Bacon, a philosopher, politician, and chief formulator of the scientific method, argued at the turn of the seventeenth century that science can and should be conducted in an objective, unbiased manner, "with minds washed clean of opinions," as he put it. Whereas a previous generation of scientists supported conclusions by noting what past authorities, such as Aristotle, the Bible, or the church, believed about the world, Bacon's scientists tried to support conclusions solely by data from the world itself. Prior beliefs, lenses, or "presuppositions" may influence interpretation, Bacon argued, and occasionally lead people astray. But through rigorous effort and self-monitoring, their influence can ultimately be minimized to obtain interpretations that provide an unbiased reflection of what the natural world is really like that every reasonable person should be able to agree upon. Thus, to take a contemporary example, Christians and non-Christians should ultimately be able to agree about the origin of human life if they don't let their prior beliefs—about the existence or nonexistence of God or the truth of the Bible, for example—influence their science.

Nineteenth-century American Christians thoroughly appropriated this philosophy, applying it to both science and biblical study. "I like a Biblical theology that does not start with . . . an hypothesis, and then warp the facts and the philosophy to fit the crook of our dogma," wrote one theologian, "but a Baconian system, which first gathers the teachings of the word of God, and then seeks to deduce some general law upon which the facts can be arranged." If nature was to be studied by clearing one's mind from all hypotheses, opinions, and the like, the Bible was to be studied by clearing one's mind from all theological beliefs and approaching the Bible to just take it for what it says, without letting lenses or biases get in the way.

Many nineteenth-century evangelicals were bothered by the diverse spectrum of opinions within the Christian community, which they blamed on all the different beliefs people brought to the Bible. If only people just took the Bible for what it says, evangelicals argued, taking off their lenses and getting back to the text itself, Christians could eventually reach a consensus and achieve unity. This approach to the Bible encouraged evangelicals to forget about what past Christians had believed; such attention to Christian tradition would only make interpreters biased in one direction or another and keep them from just taking the Bible for what it says. Allowing prior beliefs to guide interpretation, in this analysis, was to guarantee not only faulty conclusions but also factionalism and the proliferation of denominations—to guarantee, in short, a lack of consensus among Christians. This system of thought, in the words of University of Iowa historian Herbert Hovenkamp, "became an evangelical worldview that permeated every classroom and which eventually influenced hundreds of ministers, countless schoolmasters, and dozens of practicing scientists and physicians . . . [i]t became practically identified with the evangelical point of view."

This understanding of interpretation eventually caused problems for evangelicals, however, at least when it came to science. In the late 1800s, historical study began providing natural explanations for how the Bible and its doctrines were put together in history, suggesting that many stories recorded in the Bible never occurred. The theory of evolution also emerged and was used by some to argue against Christianity. Whereas science had previously been used to confirm the Bible, it was now being used to refute it. What's more, the nation's intellectual leaders—university presidents, professors, businesspeople, even many pastors—began accepting the new scientific views. Evangelicals, firmly wedded to the idea of interpretation as an objective, value-neutral enterprise, found themselves hard-pressed to reconcile their faith with these developments. At first, many evangelical leaders argued that proponents of the new scientific findings were simply biased. If the proponents were truly objective, evangelicals argued, they would reach conclusions more consistent with Christianity. But this response failed to explain why so many of the nation's intellectual leaders, many of whom began as evangelical Christians, had been convinced by the conclusions of the new science. If there was one truly objective, obvious interpretation of the science, why did so many reasonable, intelligent people fail to see it?

By the late twentieth century, such questions led many evangelicals to abandon Bacon's understanding of interpretation, at least in the realm of science. Following the Dutch theologian and politician Abraham Kuyper (1837–1920), many evangelicals began arguing that science can't be objective after all. Kuyper argued, in direct opposition to Francis Bacon, that prior beliefs cannot be brushed aside, that interpretation can't proceed without them. Everyone brings prior beliefs, presuppositions, worldviews, "interpretive paradigms," or lenses (all mean the same thing here) to the process of interpreting, he declared, and people with different ones may interpret differently as a result. If Bacon wanted everyone to take off their lenses, Kuyper declared that they can't be taken off. Kuyper even argued that there will be at least "two kinds of sciences" since Christians and non-Christians bring different assumptions to what they are interpreting. Christians and non-Christians, in this analysis, may not ultimately be able to agree about the origin of human life, since how they interpret the relevant data will be guided by prior beliefs (about the existence of God or possibility of miracles, for example).

All this is pretty abstract, so it helps to look at a concrete example of Kuyper's theory in action. A common argument for the theory of evolution is to point out that the bones in human hands are very similar to the bones in the hands of other mammals. All vertebrates, including humans, cats, whales, and bats, have a single upper arm bone, two lower arm bones, several small bones in the wrist area, and several long bones forming fingers. Why is this? Evolutionists say it is because these mammals developed from a common ancestor with that bone structure. Some bones were expanded, some reduced, and some unchanged in its descendants, but the general arrangement remained. This evidence, they say, fits perfectly with evolution. "Not so fast!" creationists respond. Sure, from an evolutionary perspective, it might seem like evidence for evolution; but this observation makes just as much sense from a creationist perspective as well. Creationists simply explain this similarity as evidence that God used the same design plan in different animals. God created humans, cats, whales, and bats with similar bones in their limbs because that was the design plan God chose. These interpretations can't be distinguished by looking harder at the bones. How the bones appear is determined by the beliefs one brings to them. This also applies to other evidence. No matter how much radiocarbon dating you show a creationist, you aren't going to convince her the earth is 4.5 billion years old if she interprets it with the belief that God created the world to look old, with the appearance of age.

By the late twentieth century, the philosophy of Kuyper had permeated evangelical thinking about science. Rather than arguing that creationism was the one, self-evident interpretation of the data, in the 1970s, creationists began insisting that schools "teach both sides"—creation science and evolution science—as two, paradigm-relative interpretations of the data. Whereas secular scientists approach the data with the presupposition that God does not exist or cannot intervene in the natural world, creationists stated that they approach it from a biblical perspective. Thus, in a 1974 article in the young earth creationist journal *Origins*, one author writes:

> All too often science is viewed as a collection of
> objective scientists: cold, calculating appraisers of
> data. . . . However, reality is somewhat different from
> that . . . scientists do not analyze data from neutral
> positions. . . . A scientist's paradigm determines
> what observations he will make, what experiments
> he will do, and how he will interpret the results of his
> experiments. . . . [T]he widely accepted concept of
> the complete objectivity of the individual scientist is
> naïve—an unfortunate twentieth century myth.

The leaders of the intelligent design (ID) movement have also adopted this understanding of interpretation, emphasizing the all-determining role of lenses or paradigms in science. Phillip Johnson, widely considered the leader of the ID movement, writes, "Every one of us has a worldview, and our worldview governs our thinking even when—or especially when—we are unaware of it." Evolution, he argues, is "based not upon any incontrovertible empirical evidence, but upon a highly philosophical presupposition." The theory of evolution, in this analysis, is simply the result of interpreting data with a non-Christian worldview.

The philosophy of Kuyper has also influenced evangelical thought about history and other areas of science. Evangelical philosopher Nicholas Wolterstorff, for example, affirms that Christians should allow their Christian convictions to shape their interpretation of scientific data, even if that means arriving at conclusions that contradict those reached by non-Christian scientists. Christian beliefs, he writes, "ought to function as a *control* over the sorts of theories which we [Christians] are willing to accept." He then provides an example of what this might look like, in the realm of psychology in this case: "Now as far as I can tell, many behaviorists and Freudians either deny human freedom and responsibility entirely, or deny them at points where Christians would affirm their presence. If so, [Christians] should reject such theories."

Likewise, evangelical philosopher Alvin Plantinga writes, "According to a popular contemporary myth, science is a cool, reasoned, wholly dispassionate attempt to figure out the truth about ourselves and our world, entirely independent of religion, or ideology, or moral convictions, or theological commitments"; "the central idea here is that science is objective, public, sharable, publicly verifiable, and equally available to anyone, whatever their religious or metaphysical proclivities"; and "I believe this view is deeply mistaken." In an article titled "Two (or More) Kinds of Scripture Scholarship," Plantinga argues against historical study used to suggest biblical stories did not actually occur. The results of such study, Plantinga states, rest on presuppositions Christians don't share— including a rejection of the supernatural—and thus should not upset Christians at all. Evangelical Bible scholar Peter Craigie explains this view well: "The principal ground of difference lies in the theological or philosophical assumptions of the starting point. These assumptions, in turn, dictate which of the possible interpretations of the data is most appropriate. . . . [A]wareness of the implications of different assumptions should introduce a more irenic attitude towards scholars with different assumptions, and consequently different interpretations of this or that set of biblical data."

While evangelicals have embraced the theory articulated by Kuyper—that interpretation can't be objective—to deal with arguments for evolution or the historical inaccuracy of the Bible, they have retained the contradictory theory articulated by Bacon—that interpretation can be objective—to maintain familiar ways of interpreting the Bible on topics like the origin of life, gender roles, or gay marrriage. As historian Mark Noll has pointed out, "Evangelicals make much of their ability to read the Bible in a 'simple,' 'literal,' or 'natural' fashion—that is, in a Baconian way. In fact, evangelical hermeneutics . . . is dictated by very specific assumptions that dominated Western intellectual life from roughly 1650 to 1850."

What this means in practice is that, when evolutionists hold up "objective facts" to challenge past ways of thinking, creationists declare that "the widely accepted concept of the complete objectivity of the individual scientist is naïve," speaking of "presuppositions," and "interpretive paradigms." When their own interpretation of the Bible is challenged, on the other hand, creationists insist they are simply maintaining an unbiased, objective, lens-free reading of "the Biblical view." As creationist Henry Morris writes, "The main reason for insisting on the universal Flood as a fact of history and as the primary vehicle for geological interpretation is that God's Word plainly teaches it! No geological difficulties, real or imagined, can be allowed to take precedence over the clear statements and necessary inferences of Scripture."

It means that when evangelical Right activists want intelligent design in public schools, they insist with Discovery Institute fellow Nancey Pearcey that "we always process data in light of some theoretical framework we have adopted for understanding the world." When they want their construal of biblical morality translated into law, on the other hand, they abandon the talk about interpretive lenses and claim objectivity, stating their moral positions are, in Pearcey's words, "based on the very Word of God, true for all times and places."

It means that when the provost of Wheaton College wants some leeway in the interpretation of the science surrounding homosexuality, he argues that scientists inescapably bring "interpretive paradigms" to the data, insisting that "more than scientific objectivity is involved in the critical evaluation of research," and stating that Christians may allow their interpretation of science to be guided by Christian theological beliefs. When he wants to fault the biblical interpretations of Christians who support gay marriage, on the other hand, he complains that they bring interpretive paradigms to the Bible rather than just taking it for what it says. Speaking of a report published by the Presbyterian Church of the USA, he protests "the authors determined that two theological/ethical concepts should drive all interpretation of the biblical witness regarding sex: *justice* and *love*. . . . This organizing rule . . . became the lens" through which this group interpreted the Bible.

It means that we find in the contemporary evangelical community two different interpretations of interpretation. In the one instance, interpretation is governed by lenses, ideology, prejudice, and the like, such that two people approaching the same data with different lenses will often interpret it in contradictory ways; disagreements cannot ultimately be settled by the data itself. In the other instance, interpretation is governed by the data itself; lenses, bias, and prejudice may exist, but their influence can ultimately be overcome or minimized, such that two people approaching the same data—regardless of how different their assumptions and biases—should ultimately be able to reach the same interpretation. The first understanding of interpretation is used to relativize challenges to conservative views from science and history. The second is employed to absolutize conservative ways of interpreting the Bible. And thus, by alternating between these two different, mutually contradictory understandings of interpretation in different contexts, familiar ways of thinking are preserved.

But if our interpretive lens is "cemented to our face," to quote Abraham Kuyper, then it cannot be taken off when we read the Bible. And thus, just as people with different interpretive lenses in the realm of science will reach different conclusions about what is scientific, people with different interpretive lenses in the realm of biblical study will reach different conclusions about what is "biblical." The practice of reading texts in their historical context is based on the realization that the meaning of any given text may be different when interpreted in light of the assumptions of ancient readers versus modern ones. Hence, a passage such as "slaves, submit to your masters" (1 Peter 2:18) takes on different meanings when read as a command in the nineteenth-century American South, an example of culturally relative ancient practices in a contemporary church, or as an allegory for how Christians should submit to the will of Christ. Like the bones in the limbs of mammals, texts take on different meanings depending on the expectations, worldviews, and assumptions one brings to them. Hence, theologians throughout history have interpreted the same verses in dramatically different, even contradictory ways, ways that directly reflect their differing worldviews and assumptions. Hence, intelligent, pious, and rigorous scholars don't agree on "what the Bible says" about gay marriage, or on the interpretation of a host of other passages, for that matter. As Merold Westphal, a philosopher at Fordham University, puts it in a 2009 book on biblical interpretation: "[O]ur interpretations are always relative to the presuppositions that we bring with us to the task of interpretation and that we have inherited and internalized from the traditions that have formed us."

What does this mean for the debate on homosexuality? Conservatives and liberals disagree about the morality of gay marriage, not because one side is biased and the other just takes the Bible for what it says, but because they bring different worldviews and assumptions to the task of biblical interpretation. These determine whether a group thinks it necessary to read texts in their historical context, what constructions of the ancient context are deemed acceptable, and how the relevance of ancient arguments about homosexuality are assessed today. They determine how willing a community is to emphasize broad themes of scripture and relativize specific commands—and for what groups a community is willing to do this. They determine what a community finds to be good analogies to homosexuality (passages on slavery and female subordination for liberals or passages on polygamy, bestiality, and incest for conservatives). They determine whether a community errs on the side of condemning activities when there is moral ambiguity or allowing them, so as to not unnecessarily restrict or oppress others. They determine whether a group thinks good interpretations of the Bible should align with popular Christian opinion or flow strictly from the work of scholars. They determine how willing one is to interpret passages allegorically versus literally, what role one thinks contemporary experience has in guiding interpretation, and how science is understood morally and related to biblical interpretation. The demographics of different communities determine which social groups contribute their perspectives to biblical interpretation and which do not. All these factors are in place before a group even looks at the Bible, and the interpretation a group reaches is a direct consequence of them.

One example of how different assumptions govern the debate over gay marriage will be instructive. The one passage in the Bible where a reason is explicitly given for the condemnation of homosexuality is in Romans 1, where the apostle Paul objects to same-sex intercourse by saying it is "unnatural." Liberal scholars point out that the only other place in the Bible where Paul invokes "nature" in his moral reasoning is in 1 Corinthians 11:7–15, where Paul writes:

> For a man ought not to have his head veiled, since he
> is the image and reflection of God; but woman is the
> reflection of man. Indeed, man was not made from
> woman, but woman from man. Neither was man
> created for the sake of woman, but woman for the
> sake of man. For this reason a woman ought to have a
> symbol of authority on her head. . . . Does not nature
> itself teach you that if a man wears long hair, it is
> degrading to him, but if a woman has long hair, it is her
> glory?

Paul's only other ethical argument from "nature" presupposes a patriarchal gender hierarchy that is disrupted by failing to conform to his culture's gender norms. Liberal scholars conclude that Paul's understanding of "nature"—and thus, both his rules about hair length and his condemnation of same-sex intercourse—is based on culturally relative views that are not held today.

Leaving aside the question of whether this argument is valid, one can point out that it rests on several assumptions not all Christians share. It assumes the reason for rules in the Bible is more important than the rules themselves. Thus, if the reason for a rule is culturally relative, the rule is culturally relative as well. It also assumes that an argument based on female subordination to men is invalid or culturally relative. Many evangelicals do not hold this view, and thus, any argument assuming it will not convince them. The debate over gay marriage ultimately hinges on different assumptions.

The relevant question in assessing evangelical thought about homosexuality, therefore, is not: Have evangelicals or liberals captured what the Bible *really* says on the matter? The relevant questions are: What cultural factors and lenses lead evangelicals to interpret the Bible as condemning gay unions? and Is there room within orthodox Christianity to approach the Bible differently?

Gay Science and Gay Politics

In assessing evangelical thought on homosexuality, it is helpful to compare it to evangelicals' thought on abortion, the other issue at the heart of their social agenda. The comparison reveals two different standards for deciding upon "the Christian position." In the case of abortion, as we saw in the previous chapter, evangelicals have happily abandoned more traditional interpretations of the Bible and embraced creative reinterpretations of all kinds to claim the Bible teaches that life begins at the moment of conception. Even while evangelicals object to appeals made to broad themes in the Bible to override the passages taken as condemning same-sex relations, they have appealed to broad themes in the Bible to override a strict construal of Exodus 21. Even while they have welcomed fallacious arguments from science to support new views on the beginning of life (claiming science proves life begins at conception, for example), they have objected to such arguments to support new views on homosexuality. Even while they object to emotional arguments from experience in the case of homosexuality, they have welcomed such arguments in the case of abortion.

This suggests that what has been the dominant evangelical social agenda for the past thirty years—with abortion and gay marriage at the center—has had less to do with defending the traditional interpretation of the Bible than with defending socially conservative cultural norms, especially those pertaining to sexuality. When more traditional interpretations of the Bible need to be abandoned to defend these norms, the necessary procedures are gladly undertaken. When more traditional interpretations of the Bible fit better with such norms, "the traditional interpretation of the Bible" is rigorously insisted upon. This suggestion receives further support from the fact that evangelicals lagged behind the broader culture on all the main social justice issues of the late twentieth century—civil rights, feminism, environmentalism—suggesting that the community has historically favored interpretations that counter social innovation.

This lagging behind the culture is demonstrated in how evangelicals have responded to the science surrounding homosexuality. When mainstream scientists believed that gay people do not choose their orientation during the 1990s, evangelical leaders were insisting that they do. As late as 2003, Focus on the Family was claiming: "There is no such thing as a homosexual. . . . We are all heterosexual." Today most evangelical leaders, even on the far right, have caught up with the culture and decided that gays don't choose to be gay after all. Asked in a 2006 interview if he still thought being gay is a choice, James Dobson responded: "I don't blame homosexuals for being angry when people say they've made a choice to be gay because they don't." The president of the Southern Baptist Convention has followed suit, proclaiming in 2007, "We sin against homosexuals by insisting that sexual temptation and attraction are predominantly chosen." (Most scientists, on the right and the left, now conclude that a homosexual orientation, like a heterosexual orientation, results from a mix of biological and environmental factors.)

When mainstream scientists believed that homosexuality is a stable orientation that is difficult if not impossible to change, evangelical organizations were promising easy conversion to heterosexuality. "We want people to know that individuals don't have to be gay," the Love Won Out conference declared, continuing on to favorably compare their efforts to a program of genocide: "The further gay argument is to say 'efforts to modify,' which is to say 'treat' Gender Identity Disorder in children is equal to 'homosexual genocide,' and they are right. It is a way to eliminate future individuals who identify as gay or lesbian." Even many far-right evangelicals are now acknowledging that a homosexual orientation is difficult and often impossible to change. Exodus International no longer promises conversions, but instead, as one of its leaders puts it, a "life of struggle with joy in the process." Such organizations now believe gays will usually remain gay, with a few fortunate exceptions; programs that once sought conversion now primarily seek to eliminate "homosexual behavior" and teach participants how to deny their sexual desire.

If evangelical interpreting on homosexuality reflects a generalized opposition to social change, it also reflects popular fears and stereotypes of gay people. A 2000 poll of small Republican donors showed that 70 percent of Republican voters involved with evangelical Christian groups would fire teachers discovered to have a gay orientation (compared with 36 percent of Republicans not involved with evangelical groups). Would they allow nonviolent demonstrations by gays and lesbians? Forty-three percent of those belonging to evangelical Christian groups would deny this constitutional right to gays and lesbians (compared with 20 percent of those not belonging to such groups). Should the government arrest homosexuals? Of the Christian Right activists surveyed, almost half answered "Yes." A 2004 National Election Study poll found that 61 percent of white evangelicals think it should be legal to discriminate against gays and lesbians on the basis of their sexual orientation. This is the culture in which evangelical scholars are interpreting their Bibles. And as Timothy Larsen, the McManis Professor of Christian Thought at Wheaton College, states of the flagship evangelical college, "Thou shalt not unsettle our constituency is the first principle around here."

These fears and prejudices are expressed in a series of internal tensions and inconsistencies in evangelical thought on homosexuality.

Profamily organizations are founded on the belief that social support is necessary for stable romantic relationships, yet they oppose social support for gay unions and then argue that gays should not be allowed to marry because their relationships are less stable than those of heterosexual couples. Evangelical leaders argue that there are "extreme variations in the cultural manifestations of homosexuality." This claim is made to downplay the role of biology in determining homosexual identity. Yet the same leaders characterize homosexuality as inherently characterized by depression, sickness, and promiscuity. Evangelical leaders regularly insist—over and against admittedly exaggerated claims that 10 percent of the population is gay—that "homosexuality almost certainly characterizes less than 3 percent (and perhaps less than 2 percent) of the population." Yet the same leaders nevertheless state that giving rights and privileges to this supposedly very, very small group will lead, in the words of Dobson, to "the utter destruction of the family" and "Western civilization itself," or even "will destroy the Earth." Lacking is any plausible explanation for how giving rights to such a small group could lead to such dramatic and devastating social change.

It is tempting to dismiss some of these points as the extreme views of the masses, irrelevant to understanding evangelical biblical scholarship. But as Mark Noll notes, "[E]vangelical interpretation assigns first place to popular approval. . . . Because of the popular traditionalism of evangelicalism as a whole . . . it has been harder for evangelical scholars to win acceptance for untraditional interpretations of Scripture than for scholars in other communities." Popular evangelical opinion—dominated by organizations such as Focus on the Family—imposes constraints on scholarly evangelical opinion. And the culture that evangelicals bring to the Bible—with its tendency to resist social change, its stereotypes and fears of gays and lesbians, its tolerance of pseudoscience, and its preference for simple and uncomplicated readings—constrains how they interpret it.

Loving the Sinner

A popular refrain in the gay debate is that Christians are to love homosexuals—but hate their sin. This seems like a moderate position to many evangelicals, familiar with a generation that hated the sin and hated the homosexual as well. Unfortunately, by presenting "love" as simply a matter of applying a given set of rules kindly, this maxim ignores the fact that sometimes love requires questioning the rules themselves. The origin of the maxim demonstrates as much. It is not from the Bible but the work of Augustine. He articulated this concept in a letter to a group of nuns, and the sins for which he chastised them included their wish for more frequent baths, their storage of gifts sent from home, and their failure to keep their hair concealed by a habit. To many evangelicals, "love the sinner, hate the sin" means that Christians are to assume current interpretations of the Bible are correct and, even while enforcing the interpretations nicely, be unwilling to seriously consider arguments against them. Any attempt to reconsider past moral judgments in light of new evidence about the ancient meaning of the biblical texts, arguments about the moral relevance of science, or experiences of gays and lesbians, in the minds of many evangelicals, can only be an attempt to rationalize sin. But Augustine's injunction to the nuns demonstrates the limits of this mentality. Part of "loving the sinner" must be making sure that legitimate desires and activities are not unjustly classified as "sin."

The general approach of evangelicals in the debate on gay marriage has paralleled the approach of an earlier generation of evangelicals, young earth creationists, in the debate over evolution (a topic covered in chapter 5). In both cases, evangelicals have brought a particular understanding of the Bible into the flux of contemporary experience and insisted it just has to cohere with that experience—it must be scientifically valid in the one case or the loving thing to do in the other—because otherwise they won't be believing the Bible. Creationists understand the Bible as saying the earth is only a few thousand years old so they must interpret science accordingly, no matter how much selectivity or manipulation it requires. Opponents of gay marriage understand the Bible as condemning it so they must interpret its prohibition as the loving thing to do, regardless of its observable impact on the lives of gays and lesbians. In both cases, evangelicals have ignored the manner in which their construal of "the Bible" is determined by a particular cultural location and lens and how bringing different beliefs to the text would lead to a different construal of what the Bible says, one that does not require manipulation, distortion, or denial of our experiences of the world around us (as in the pseudoscientific ventures of creationists or the trivialization of gay/lesbian experiences by opponents of gay marriage). Put differently, evangelicals have not considered that, if what we think the Bible says clashes significantly with what we experience today, we may not be interpreting the Bible properly.

If Augustine gives Christians an often problematically applied maxim, he also gives them a solution to this interpretive trend. In response to the creationists of his day, Augustine insisted that scientific knowledge of the world must inform the interpretation of Scripture. His primary concern was the negative impact such endeavors had on evangelism:

> Usually, even a non-Christian knows something,
> about the earth, the heavens, and the other elements of
> this world . . . and this knowledge he holds to as
> being certain from reason and experience. Now, it
> is a disgraceful and dangerous thing for an infidel to
> hear a Christian, presumably giving the meaning of
> Holy Scripture, talking nonsense on these topics. . . .
> If they find a Christian mistaken in a field which they
> themselves know well and hear him maintaining
> his foolish opinions about our books, how are they
> going to believe those books in matters concerning
> the resurrection of the dead, the hope of eternal

> life, and the kingdom of heaven, when they think
> their pages are full of falsehoods on facts which they
> themselves have learnt from experience and the light
> of reason.

Sound biblical interpretations cannot ignore our experiences of the world around us, in this analysis.

Likewise, in deciding how to construe "biblical morality," Augustine insists that the impact of the interpretation on others must be considered: "Whoever, therefore, thinks that he understands the divine Scriptures or any part of them so that it does not build the double love of God and of our neighbor does not understand it at all." Augustine states that passages should be read figuratively if a literal reading does not promote love for others: "If scripture seems to advocate love, it is literal; if it seems to advocate malice, it is figurative." Such interpretations are true, in his reckoning, regardless of what the author intended: "Whoever finds a lesson there useful to the building of charity, even though he has not said what the author may be shown to have intended in that place, has not been deceived, nor is he lying in any way."

There is ample room within the diverse interpretive practices of orthodox Christianity to justify an alternative approach to the Bible on gay marriage. Defending the exclusion of gays from marriage, therefore, is not ultimately about defending the Bible. It is about defending the unacknowledged lenses, cultural values, and fears of its interpreters. Throughout their history in the late twentieth century, evangelicals were consistently on the side of those holding back justice, dismissing the civil rights movement, opposing the feminist movement, and harboring unwarranted skepticism for the environmental movement. This track record has irreparably damaged the credibility of evangelicals in the secular American culture—and undermined willingness of those who are not Christians to receive the gospel they preach. Evangelicals may lament this history, but they have done little to change the intellectual habits and social structures responsible for it. The movement for gay marriage provides an opportunity for this change to occur. Given their insistence on the role of lenses and paradigms in interpretation, evangelicals can no longer plausibly claim to be held back by the Bible. Indeed, the evangelical case against gay marriage is based on an understanding of interpretation that evangelicals elsewhere reject. The only things holding evangelicals back from embracing justice for gays and lesbians are evangelicals themselves.

FOUR

Environmental Experiences:
Global Warming, Stewardship, and Traditional Christian
Antienvironmentalism

A GROUP OF CHRISTIAN LEADERS gathered in the rolling green hills of Cornwall, Connecticut, in the fall of 1999 for an important meeting. Charles Colson, Donald Wildmon, and James Dobson, among others came together to address a growing threat to America. In this case, however, it was not the prospect of gay people marrying each other. In fact, this time, the threat was so insidious that even evangelical Christians were falling prey.

That threat was the environmental movement. In a document by the group, titled *The Cornwall Declaration on Environmental Stewardship*, those present condemned environmentalism as "based on a romantic view of nature, a misguided distrust of science and technology, and an intense focus on problems that are highly speculative." Concerns raised by environmentalists were dismissed as baseless and extreme. The document concludes with an affirmation of the importance of free-market capitalism and the need to let it operate without major constraints.

Despite the efforts of the group, by February of 2007, its worst fears were realized. The environmental movement had infiltrated evangelical Christianity. Richard Cizik, vice president of the National Association of Evangelicals, which lobbies the government on behalf of evangelicals across America, had made public his belief that global warming is partly

caused by human activity. Many of the same leaders regathered to produce another document, a letter to the NAE demanding that Cizik either
abandon his views about global warming or resign. "Cizik and others," the
letter read, "are using the global warming controversy to shift emphasis
away from the great moral issues of our time," referring to homosexuality and abortion. "The existence of global warming and its implications
for mankind is a subject of heated controversy," the authors continued. "If
he cannot be trusted to articulate the views of American evangelicals on
environmental issues, then we respectfully suggest that he be encouraged
to resign his position with the NAE."

In December of 2008, after twenty-eight years of service, Richard
Cizik was indeed forced to resign. His resignation did not only result
from his views on global warming. In a 2008 interview he also noted his
support for civil unions for gay couples. But the *Cornwall* team took it as
a victory nonetheless. "This sends the message," Tony Perkins of the Family Research Council declared, that deviation from a strict antiabortion/
antihomosexuality issue agenda will be punished. And indeed it was.

Despite the transition toward a greener evangelicalism represented
by Cizik and an increasingly large number of evangelicals across America,
the antienvironmental advocacy of Charles Colson and company re-
calls a darker, more ambiguous part of Christian history. Indeed, the
dim view of the environment present throughout Christian tradition
has prompted many observers to suggest that Christianity is itself a primary cause of the environmental crisis today—that the Bible, in short,
is antienvironmental. To understand the appeal of this view, one needs
only look to the best-selling Left Behind series (written by Tim LaHaye
and Jerry Jenkins), which directs Bible-believing Christians to look forward to their evacuation from this world, which, in any case, will be
destroyed when Jesus returns. Evangelicals have gotten this idea, in part,
from their interpretation of 2 Peter 3:10, which states, "But the day of

the Lord will come like a thief. The heavens will disappear with a roar; the elements will be destroyed by fire, and the earth and everything in it will be laid bare." The consequences of this interpretation for the environment were most famously displayed by James G. Watt, Ronald Reagan's evangelical Christian secretary of the interior—"arguably the most anti-environmental secretary ever" in the opinion of the Audubon Society—who declared "we will mine more, drill more, cut more timber" because "I don't know how many future generations we can count on before the Lord returns."

Apart from its expectations of the imminent destruction of the earth, proenvironment critics of the Bible point to the command in Genesis 1:28 to "be fruitful and multiply it" and "have dominion over the beasts." The full text reads:

> God blessed them, and God said to them, "Be fruitful
> and multiply, and fill the earth and subdue it; and
> have dominion over the fish of the sea and over the
> birds of the air and over every living thing that moves
> upon the earth."

The Bible, according to some interpreters of this verse, informs humans they should continually reproduce without regard for environmental limitations, are superior to the rest of the biological world, and have a divinely ordained duty to exploit it for their own welfare. Environmentalists certainly aren't dissuaded from these conclusions when they hear evangelical leaders, such as E. Calvin Beisner of the Cornwall Alliance, declare: "Biblical Christians . . . can have confidence that, by the grace of God through the death, resurrection, and ascension of Christ and His present reign over all things, continued populated growth will result not in the depletion but in the increased abundance of resources, and not in the increased pollution of the earth but in its increased cleansing and transformation."

Late-twentieth-century evangelicals, in particular, resisted the environmental movement because of their alliance with the Republican Party. Ross Douthat, a conservative *New York Times* columnist, explains why. Speaking of the decade when right-wing politics emerged, he notes:

> The Seventies were a great decade for apocalyptic
> enthusiasms, and none was more potent than the
> fear that human population growth had outstripped
> the earth's carrying capacity. According to a chorus
> of credentialed alarmists, the world was entering an
> age of sweeping famines, crippling energy shortages,
> and looming civilizational collapse. It was not lost
> on conservatives that this analysis led inexorably to
> left-wing policy prescriptions—a government-run
> energy sector at home, and population control for the
> teeming masses overseas. . . . And time was unkind to
> the alarmists. The catastrophes never materialized. . . .
> This is the lens through which most conservatives
> view the global warming debate. Again, a doomsday
> scenario has generated a crisis atmosphere, which is
> being invoked to justify taxes and regulations that many
> left-wingers would support anyway.

To politically conservative evangelicals, environmental crises—described by scientists who overwhelmingly fall on the politically liberal side of the spectrum—seem a little too convenient for the party they oppose.

Nevertheless, despite the Cornwall Declaration, and forced resignation of Cizik, despite the Left Behind series, despite the dominion mandate and left-wing policy prescriptions, proenvironment views are becoming increasingly common in the evangelical community. Whereas a previous generation of evangelicals constituted one of the largest antienvironmentalist forces, a substantial number have rallied behind the cause today. This change is apparent, among other places, in a string of proenvironmental declarations released over the past fifteen years: *An Evangelical Declaration on the Care of Creation* in 1994, *For the Health of the Nations* released by the National Association of Evangelicals in 2004, and the *Evangelical Climate Initiative* in 2006, signed by evangelical leaders across the political spectrum. Even the right-wing Southern Baptist Convention has begun to join the cause, with a 2008 resolution stating: "The time for timidity regarding God's creation is no more."

Against past apathy of evangelicals, these Christian environmentalists have looked to the Bible as clearly mandating care for creation. As *Christianity Today* puts it, "The Bible is not an enemy of the environmental cause, but its greatest asset." What about the earth being destroyed when Jesus returns? These green evangelicals believe the earth will actually be redeemed. Instead of focusing on 2 Peter 3:10 and its promise that "the heavens will disappear" at the end of time, green evangelicals focus on Romans 8:21's statement that "creation itself will be liberated from its bondage to decay and brought into the glorious freedom of the children of God." According to evangelical environmentalist R. J. Berry, Romans 8:21 "clearly speaks of renewal rather than replacement." And if this world will be renewed at the end of time, then the popular song is wrong. This world is our home, and we're not just passing through. What about the Genesis 1:28 command to "subdue the earth"? These evangelical environmentalists prefer Genesis 2:15, where Adam is instructed to "till and keep" the Garden of Eden. Genesis 1:28, they say, should be interpreted through the lens of Genesis 2:15, not vice versa. As Calvin DeWitt writes, "In the context of the rest of the Bible . . . one must come to the conclusion that dominion means responsible stewardship." Humans are to take care of the world, in this analysis, not exploit it. Ron Sider, founder of Evangelicals for Social Action, sums up the overall argument of green evangelicals well: "Many Christians who are not environmentalists . . . have not carefully attended to what the Bible says."

But not every observer of the Christian environmental movement is convinced. Thomas Derr, currently a professor emeritus of religion and ethics at Smith College, though aiming at liberal Protestants, raises a concern that can be applied to green evangelicals as well. He asks, "What motivates Protestant eco-theologians as they rummage through the Bible. . . . how much their ecological agenda directs their search for support in the Bible."

Through all the intricate, complex biblical arguments, through all the insistences that Bible readers should focus on this verse over here and not that one over there, it's easy to empathize with Derr's bemusement. One can come away with a sense that green readings involve more than a passive "listening" to scripture. Indeed, one may sense that, rather than discovering a green Bible, evangelical environmentalists are creating a green Bible. That's because evangelicals have embraced environmentalism, not because they've finally discovered what the Bible really says about the matter, but because they've reinterpreted the Bible in light of their experience of the environmental crisis.

The Bible Isn't Pro-Environmental

The selectivity of green readings of scripture is demonstrated by focusing on passages these readings downplay or ignore. Aside from the Genesis 1:28 command to "subdue" the earth (which, in the original language, literally means "conquer" or "trample"), the God of the Old Testament regularly destroys the environment to punish humans. Noah's flood is one example, where, in response to human immorality, God sends rain that kills millions of animals and plants. But we also find God destroying portions of the Earth in numerous other passages (Amos 9:5–6, Isaiah 24:4

"See, the LORD is going to lay waste to the earth and devastate it . . .").
The Earth may be "very good," and may ultimately belong to God, as we
learn in Genesis 1 and Psalm 24. But that doesn't stop God from cursing
the Earth after Adam and Eve sin. And, in any case, in Psalm 115:16, we
learn that God has "given [the Earth] to man." The Old Testament commanded Israelites to slaughter animals in hundreds of situations. A skin infection, for example, requires killing one dove and a lamb (Leviticus 14).

The New Testament has similar material. Jesus allows a demon to
kill a herd of pigs (Matthew 8:28–34) and informs his human followers that birds are much less important than they themselves are (Luke
12:6–7). Plants don't fare any better; Jesus kills a fig tree because it isn't
bearing fruit, though the gospel writer notes "it was not the season for
figs" (Matthew 21:18–22, Mark 11:23–14), and Jesus tells his disciples
that God is much more concerned about them than plants (Matthew
6:25–34). After noting the Old Testament proscription "You shall not
muzzle an ox while it is treading out the grain," the Apostle Paul asks in
1 Corinthians 9:9–10: "Is it for oxen that God is concerned? Or does he
not speak entirely for our sake?" Paul concludes, "It was indeed written
for our sake."

In light of such passages, it's not difficult to see why nearly all theologians prior to the late twentieth century read their Bibles in ways that
would make the Audubon Society cringe. To be sure, there are some exceptions to this tradition. Augustine condemns the "lust to dominate"
as sinful and suggests the natural world also exists to praise God. Saint
Francis of Assisi is famous for spending his days with animals. And the Reformers, Calvin and Luther, often suggest that God's glory is expressed in
nature, with Calvin insisting that humans should care for nature like they
care for their other possessions.

But these exceptions pale in comparison to the overwhelmingly
dominant consensus that nature has little value, if any, apart from its use-
fulness for humans. Augustine wrote that man "is a rational animal, and

consequently more excellent than all other animals of the earth." Animals are therefore, he continues, "subject to our use." Augustine pointed to the Gospels to support his view, noting the pig and fig tree episodes to downplay the value of nonhuman life. Aquinas reaffirmed Augustine's views, declaring, "The whole of material nature exists for man. . . . The life of animals and plants is preserved not for themselves but for man." Animal abuse is not inherently wrong, in Aquinas's analysis, but only wrong insofar as it can lead its practitioners to treat humans poorly. His contemporary, Hildegard of Bingen, added, "Man sits on the judgement [sic] seat of the word. He rules over creation. Each creature is under his control and in his service. He is above all other creatures." The medieval theologian Bonaventure agreed: "We are the end of all things that exist . . . all corporeal beings are made for the service of man." Even Francis of Assisi, often held up as the patron saint of ecologists, believed that "every creature proclaims: 'God made me for your sake, O man!'"

Continuing in this tradition, John Calvin likened natural objects to material possessions that were given by God to humans. Calvin writes that the "end for which all things were created [was] that none of the conveniences and necessities of life might be wanting to men." Martin Luther agreed, averring that the Bible "plainly teaches that God created all these things . . . for the future of man . . . night and day alternate for the purpose of refreshing our bodies by rest. The sun shines that work may be done. . . . The animals are subjected to man as to a tyrant who has absolute power over life and death."

And this is to say nothing of the sentiments expressed by evangelicals throughout the twentieth century. One study found that Christians with the "highest" view of the Bible—as 100 percent true, with no errors—were the least likely to care about the environment. An independent study came to a similar conclusion: "Evangelical self-identification is strongly associated with less support for the environment." According to a 2007 Barna poll, "Evangelicals stood out regarding their views on the environment. Only 35% said that protecting the environment should be a top priority—the lowest score recorded among any of the 80 subgroups studied. The national average was 60%." What is the most Bible-focused group in America is, according to these studies, also the least likely group in America to care about ecological matters. Obviously, we wouldn't expect this if, as one prominent evangelical environmentalist declares, "The Bible has a deceptively simple and clear-cut concept of creation care."

Despite such statistics, and despite hundreds of years of biblical interpretations with sorry implications for the environment, promulgated by the most esteemed theologians and biblical interpreters, along come progressive evangelicals, shortly after a major environmental crisis, and claim the Bible's quite clearly been green all along. Augustine, Aquinas, Calvin, Luther, and evangelicals throughout the twentieth century carried on their views—they just didn't read their Bibles closely enough. *Christianity Today* may claim that the Bible is the "greatest asset" to the environmental movement. But the Bible is only an asset to the environmental movement if it is read with a lens that yields a proenvironmental reading. And for most of Christian history, it was not read with such a lens.

The Bible Isn't Anti-Environmental

In light of the history of biblical interpretation on the matter, many secularists understandably believe the Bible is inherently antienvironmental. After all, how can you get around a command like that found in Genesis 1:28: "Be fruitful and multiply, and fill the earth and subdue it; and have dominion over the fish of the sea and over the birds of the air and over every living thing that moves upon the earth"? Green evangelicals may claim that Genesis 1:28—the verse at the center of the debate over Christianity and the environment—really commands Christians to exercise "stewardship," to care for the environment and protect it from abuse. But the word "stewardship" is not found in the Bible in discussions of nature and it was not widely used to interpret Genesis 1:28 until the 1600s, as we will see.

During four different eras of history, as Peter Harrison, a professor of science and religion at Oxford University has helped demonstrate, Christians have interpreted the command to exercise "dominion" in very different, even mutually contradictory ways, ways that directly reflect their different cultural situations and theological beliefs. Surveying each era's interpretation demonstrates that the Bible isn't proenvironmental, and it's not antienvironmental either, because what the Bible is reflects the beliefs we bring to it.

CONTROLLING THE PASSIONS

Due to the prevalence of allegorical interpretation at the time, and also the stress on asceticism, the church fathers—including Origen, Augustine, Jerome, and John Chrysostom, among others—viewed the Genesis 1:28 command to "have dominion over the beasts" as a command to control their own passions and lusts. A popular belief at the time, Harrison notes, was that the human body is like a miniature world. The "beasts" of Genesis 1:28 were taken as referring to passions, lusts, and impulses within the body. The theologian Origen, for example, described human passions as analogous to "herds of cattle," "birds of the air," and "flocks of sheep and flocks of goats." The fall of mankind into sin was thought to result in reason's loss of control over passion: by "having dominion" over that passion, these interpreters hoped to return internally to the original, perfected state. Thus, Augustine took the "beasts" as referring to "the affections of the soul," which could "serve reason when they are restrained from their deathly ways." And likewise, John Chrysostom affirmed that Christians must "control and tame" our ideas and passions ("brute beasts," he calls them) and "submit them to the rule of reason." Harrison summarizes: "The imperative force of the biblical injunction 'have dominion' thus became, during the patristic era, a powerful incentive to bring rebellious carnal impulses under the control of reason."

HUMAN ENCYCLOPEDIAS

In the medieval era, another interpretation arose. The stage was set for a new interpretation of Genesis 1:28 by a translation of the works of Aristotle into Latin. Aristotle's works contained encyclopedia-like descriptions of objects in the natural world and spurned an interest in comprehensive bodies of knowledge, particularly about nature. Indeed, the comprehensive way in which Aristotle set forth and described various animals and plants in the natural world, pointing out their relations to each other, the logic governing their activities, and physical resemblances, made nature seem like a book, with an internal grammar that could be elucidated through careful study. The idea of a "book of nature," Harrison writes, "implied that that world, like scripture, was a locus of divine revelation, and potentially both a source of knowledge of God and a means by which mankind might be reconciled to him. Nature was a new authority, an alternative text, a doorway to the divine which could stand alongside the sacred page."

Whereas the fall of humankind into sin was thought by patristic theologians to obliterate the control of passion by reason, medieval theologians understood it as leading to a loss of the comprehensive, encyclopedic knowledge once possessed by Adam (his naming of animals in Genesis was taken by many to indicate his comprehensive knowledge). The Genesis 1:28 command to "subdue the Earth" and "have dominion" over the beasts was thus interpreted as commanding Christians to regain the encyclopedic knowledge lost by Adam in the Fall, thus restoring the original, perfected state. Medieval theologian Bonaventure, for example, declared that before Adam's fall, Adam "possessed knowledge of created things and was raised through their representation to God and his praise."

By regaining this knowledge, humans "are led back to God." As Harrison notes, "Knowledge of the creatures was thus another way of restoring, in a fashion, the original dominion that the human race had once enjoyed." If the command to "have dominion" was a moral imperative during the patristic era, during the medieval era, it was an intellectual imperative, a command to study the world. Yet the command did not direct readers to the empirical world itself, but to the world as described in books and by past authorities (such as Aristotle).

THE INVENTION OF ENVIRONMENTAL STEWARDSHIP

Things changed with the Protestant Reformation. With a desire for an unambiguous authority to hold up over the Catholic Church, the Reformers championed the "literal sense" of the Bible and mostly abandoned both allegorical interpretation—which previously had complemented literalism as a mode of interpretation—and the idea that past authorities, or "tradition," should govern biblical interpretation. As Harrison argues, this had significant ramifications for the environment. For one thing, it contributed to the mentality that led to the emergence of modern science and technology. If Christians were to be chastised for going to the Bible as mediated by tradition, rather than the Bible itself, scientists were soon chastised for studying nature as mediated by tradition, rather than nature itself. Francis Bacon thus wrote in the 1600s: "In the inquiry of divine truth" scholars are "ever inclined to leave the oracles of God's word [so in the] inquisition of nature they have ever left the oracles of God's works." Whereas scientists had once studied nature mostly by examining what various authorities—Aristotle, the Bible, theologians—said about it, they now studied nature empirically, conducting experiments and accepting conclusions without regard to what past authorities believed.

For another thing, the insistence on "the Bible alone" and "the literal sense" meant that Genesis 1:28 was now construed literally. If church fathers gave it a moral interpretation, as a command to control the passions with reason; if medieval theologians gave it an intellectual interpretation, as a command to regain the encyclopedic knowledge lost in the Fall; Protestant Christians gave it a physical interpretation. Scientists sought to regain the physical rule over the world that Adam was thought to enjoy before his fall into sin. As Bacon declared: "For man by the fall fell at the same time from this state of innocency and from his dominion over creation. Both of these losses however can even in this life be in some part repaired; the former by religion and faith, the latter by arts and sciences." Driven by Bacon's interpretation of Genesis and his philosophy, the newly developing science sought to elucidate nature's laws so that humans could manipulate it for their benefit.

It was in this context that the concept of exercising "stewardship" over the environment was created. Although ideas similar to that of stewardship could be found in Augustine, Benedictine monks, and John Calvin, among others, the concept was first systematically set forth and widely accepted in the 1600s. "Stewardship" served as a counterpart to the new scientific zeal for manipulating nature for human benefit, suggesting that humans had a duty not only to themselves, but to the natural world as well. A widely accepted belief at the time, based on a literal construal of Genesis 3:17–19, was that the entire earth was cursed as a result of human sin, turning it from order to disorder; from fertility to infertility; from a smooth surface to one ravaged by valleys and mountains; from harmony and peace between animals to strife and warfare. Nature, untouched by humans, was not regarded as "natural," or pure and pristine as it is today. It was regarded as devastated by sin and in need of reordering.

The seventeenth-century concept of exercising "stewardship" over the environment involved the idea that humans should intervene in nature in order to improve it, returning it to its "natural," ordered state. Matthew Hale, the chief justice of England, set forth the concept in a 1677 treatise: "In relation to this inferior World . . . [man] should be the VICE-ROY of the great God of Heaven and Earth in this inferior World;

his Steward . . . of this inferior World to husband and order it . . . to correct the redundance [*sic*] of unprofitable vegetables . . . and render the Earth more beautiful and useful." By intervening in nature to improve it, seventeenth-century stewards believed they were redeeming the world. Thus, this mentality was consistent with the idea that the earth will be redeemed at the end of time; these "stewards" felt they were anticipating that redemption now through rigorous intervention in the natural world. As one author wrote, "A skilful and industrious improvement of the creatures [will lead to] a fuller taste of Christ and Heaven."

In addition to justifying human intervention in the environment, Harrison notes that the seventeenth-century concept of "environmental stewardship" was also bound up with the understanding of property. In this analysis, if you failed to modify the land you inhabited, to exercise "stewardship," you didn't really own it. As philosopher John Locke explained: "God and his reason commanded him to subdue the earth, i.e. improve it for the benefit of life. . . . He that in obedience to this command of God, subdued, tilled, and sowed any part of it, thereby annexed to it something that was his property." This interpretation of Genesis 1:28 provided a major justification for the displacement—and in some cases, slaughter—of the native inhabitants of America, who had not properly exercised "stewardship" over their natural surroundings.

This is the understanding of "environmental stewardship" that is championed today by evangelical antienvironmentalists. E. Calvin Beisner, a professor at Covenant College and leader of the Cornwall Alliance, writes, "[T]he desire to keep large tracts of land . . . in the wild, natural state, unchanged by humanity, is . . . unbiblical, in that it contradicts the dominion mandate." God "gave man a stewardly responsibility to subdue and rule the earth (Genesis 1:26–28), and when He placed man in the Garden of Eden, He instructed him to cultivate and guard it

(Genesis 2:15), implying that it is right and good in principle for people to interfere with nature." Against many evangelical environmentalists, who suggest that humans are commanded in Genesis 2:15 to "till and keep" the earth (and thus, that "dominion" really means to care for the earth), Beisner writes, "[T]he Biblical text makes it quite clear that the Garden Adam was told to till and keep was not the same as the earth he was told to subdue and rule. . . . It was specifically the *Garden* that Adam was to till and keep (2:15). In contrast, it was the *earth* that he was to subdue and rule (1:28). . . . Adam's dominion mandate involved his transforming, bit by bit, the rest of the earth from glory to glory." Like the seventeenth-century stewards, Beisner believes the entire earth will be redeemed at the end of time; he simply believes that human reordering of nature anticipates that redemption today.

THE REINVENTION OF ENVIRONMENTAL STEWARDSHIP

Although the seventeenth-century understanding of "environmental stewardship" persists in the work of Beisner and others today, it is no longer the mainstream understanding. Clare Palmer, a professor of philosophy and environmental studies at Washington University, has argued that the currently popular understanding of "stewardship"—that humans are to care for nature and protect it from abuse—arose in part from financial problems in churches in the mid-1900s. A popular way of framing church-based fund-raising appeals was to say Christians must use their money wisely because it really belongs to God. "There is only one legitimate answer to the financial problem," *The Christian Century* declared in 1950, to "teach our people to practice Christian stewardship." The environmental crisis came to light in the midst of these appeals. And in 1967, historian Lynn White published a famous article declaring that the Christian idea of "dominion" (in Genesis 1:28) was largely to blame.

"Christianity," White wrote, "not only established a dualism of man and nature, but also insisted that it is God's will that man exploit nature for his proper ends."

Christians seeking to counter White's thesis and vindicate the Bible in the face of a growing environmental crisis extended the financial understanding of "stewardship" to include the natural world. As Palmer argues:

> It was probably this availability of the metaphor [i.e., stewardship] that first led to its wide application to the natural world. It could easily be extended from money, talents and human resources, to refer to (so called) natural resources. . . . [By] the use of the word "steward", the natural world is linked to money and resources. . . . We are here to look after it, cultivate it, develop it, use it—but prudently. . . . We must not destroy it by "spending it all at once."

Thus, Christian apologists decided that "dominion" (in Genesis 1:28) really means "stewardship," drawing on the Genesis 2:15 command to "till and keep" the earth as specifying the *real* meaning of "dominion" in Genesis 1:28. With this new understanding, "environmental stewardship" usually did not involve intervening in nature and making it more orderly and useful, as it had in the seventeenth century. Now "environmental stewardship" generally meant refraining from intervention in nature and shielding it from human abuse.

Although mainline Christians generally led the way in proenvironment advocacy, evangelical Christians (contrary to popular perceptions) were quite receptive to environmentalism initially. In 1970, the National Association of Evangelicals declared that those who "thoughtlessly destroy a God-ordained balance of nature are guilty of sin against God's creation." *Christianity Today* decried environmentally insensitive practices, as did *Moody Monthly* and *Christian Life*.

Nevertheless, as the 1970s progressed and the evangelical Right emerged, evangelical Christianity became increasingly Republican. By 1973, *Christianity Today* was showing skepticism toward the idea of "environmental stewardship." The general attitude of complacency could be summarized by the title of an article written by the magazine's editor: "To Live Is to Pollute." In the mind of one columnist, encouraging obedience to the Bible, not stewardship of nature, should be the top priority for Christians (apparently, the two were unrelated). According to a 1978 piece by the editor of *Christian Life*, "The environmental problem is not as significant as many people think."

Although these attitudes persist in the evangelical community to this day, the initial ember of proenvironment sentiment never died out. Over the 1977–78 school year, Calvin College sponsored a forum on "Christian Stewardship and Natural Resources," culminating in the publication of *Earthkeeping: Christian Stewardship of Natural Resources*. The Au Sable Institute, an evangelical environmental learning center, was founded in 1978 and rose to prominence during the 1980s. And in 1994, evangelicals came together to issue *An Evangelical Declaration on the Care of Creation*, discussing "the biblical principles of stewardship" (with "stewardship" defined in the new, post-1970s sense) and repenting for having "failed in our stewardship of creation" in the past.

Many progressive evangelicals have supported the embrace of environmentalism by claiming that this teaching has been sitting in the pages of scripture since scripture was written. R. J. Berry, for example, writes about "the historical Christian doctrine that we are stewards of creation," suggesting the Bible has taught the contemporary understanding of stewardship all along. This assumes that virtually all past Christians—

who did not generally interpret the Bible this way—were misreading the text and that Christians have only discovered what the Bible really says on the environment in the late twentieth century, after a major environmental crisis. But what changed from era to era was not the Bible, or even knowledge about the ancient meaning of the text; it was the culture, assumptions, and experiences of its interpreters. Each era's interpretations can be traced directly to these factors, including the interpretations of contemporary evangelicals.

Some evangelicals have acknowledged as much, stating that experiences have played a determining role in their embrace of green views. Richard Cizik, for example, writes, in an article about why he changed his mind, "What got my attention, and keeps it, is the impact of climate change, habitat destruction, and species extinction on Earth." He reiterates, "It took the unequivocal evidence of climate change . . . to shake me out of my own lethargy." Likewise, Steven Bouma-Prediger, a theologian at Hope College, states: "[M]y readings are informed by what we know of how the world works and of what is currently wrong. My reading, in other words, is unapologetically informed by ecology and, more exactly, by the challenges we face as we attempt to be faithful followers of Jesus in an ecologically imperiled age." What these Christians recognize is what the history of the interpretation of Genesis 1:28 shows: Evangelicals have turned green because of their environmental experiences.

Environmental Experiences

The fact that the Bible's meaning is not simply lying in its pages waiting to be discovered, but rather, occurs at the intersection of scripture, theology, and culture, necessitates a change in the way evangelicals use and think about scripture. No longer can it be viewed as a receptacle of answers, waiting to dragged out and applied to questions today. No longer can the Bible be understood as an active agent that dispenses its own interpretations—at least to those unbiased enough to listen. Biases and prior beliefs are not something that get in the way of interpretation, something that must be brushed aside; rather, biases and prior beliefs are behind every interpretation. They are necessary for interpretation to occur at all. In this light, the focus of debates over the Bible must shift to questions of how Christians *should* interpret, reflecting a realization that humans have a choice in the matter and the Bible can't answer the question for us. Evangelicals should acknowledge that contemporary experiences are a legitimate guide to interpreting scripture, in short, because contemporary experiences already undergrid how evangelicals interpret scripture.

In light of their experiences of the environmental crisis, green evangelicals have reinterpreted the Bible in an environmentally friendly way. Why have evangelicals changed their minds? Harvard Medical School's Eric Chivian eloquently summarizes some of the reasons in a 2009 appeal to evangelical Christians:

> Because the World Health Organization estimates that climate change already claims over 150,000 lives each year from storms, droughts, and famines, and predicts that these figures will grow exponentially in coming decades, with the poorest among us being the most vulnerable.
>
> Because heat waves, like the one in Europe during August of 2003 that killed as many as 35,000 people will become increasingly numerous, longer in duration, and lethal, especially in urban centers around the world, with infants and children, the elderly, the homeless, and the chronically ill at the greatest risk.
>
> Because deadlier storms and hurricanes will injure and kill increasing numbers on land and at sea.
>
> Because droughts and excessive heat, flooding,

and sea level rise will cause extensive crop failures and famine, will drastically reduce drinking water supplies and massively increase the numbers of environmental refugees, estimated to reach hundreds of millions and perhaps even 1 billion people by 2050, and will cause increased conflict, such as is now occurring in Darfur.

Because climate change will increase outbreaks and the spread of some human infectious diseases like cholera, malaria, dengue fever, and schistosomiasis.

Because it will endanger the survival of millions of plant, animal, and microbial species, potentially disrupting ecosystems in ways that may threaten their life support functioning, in ways we now barely understand.

If one accepts these scientific claims—and, after years of resistance and denial, most mainstream evangelical leaders now do—it becomes hard to claim that Christianity is good news for the culture if it can't help solve these problems. And it becomes even harder to claim it is good news if it exacerbates them. It also becomes hard to interpret the Bible the way it used to be interpreted. Experiences, like that of the environmental crisis, are a valid reason for reinterpreting the Bible—even if it means departing from centuries of more traditional interpretations in the process.

Evolving Evangelicals:
Creationism, Intelligent Design,
and Keeping an Open Mind

FOR MANY EVANGELICALS, AT the end of the day, all the main problems with contemporary culture—including abortion, homosexuality, and Earth worship, among others—can be traced to the theory of evolution. Many evangelicals believe that if evolution is true, God isn't. And if that's the case, since God is the author of morality, no morals exist either, in this analysis. What's more, if humans aren't really made in God's image, they aren't that special after all, many believe. Perhaps Friedrich Nietzsche, a contemporary of Darwin's, put the problem best: "We wished to awaken the feeling of man's sovereignty by showing his divine birth; this path is now forbidden, since a monkey stands at the entrance." It's only a short step from these beliefs, in the minds of many Christians, to the immorality and degrading of human life evangelicals see exemplified by abortion, gay marriage, and the environmental movement—and indeed, to the downfall of Western civilization itself.

These sentiments are hardly unique. For many opponents of evolution, the widespread acceptance of evolution is the cause of just about everything else that is wrong with the world. As we read in the infamous "Wedge Document," a founding document of the intelligent design movement:

111

The proposition that human beings are created in
the image of God is one of the bedrock principles on
which Western civilization was built. . . . Yet little over
a century ago, this cardinal idea came under wholesale
attack by intellectuals drawing on the discoveries
of modern science. . . . [T]hinkers such as Charles
Darwin, Karl Marx, and Sigmund Freud portrayed
humans not as moral and spiritual beings, but as
animals or machines who inhabited a universe ruled
by purely impersonal forces. . . . This materialistic
conception of reality eventually infected virtually every
area of our culture.

Similar convictions are artfully expressed in diagrams commonly
made by young earth creationists that contrast the supposed implications
of creation with evolution. The diagrams feature two books, one titled *The
Word of God,* the other titled *The Mind of Man.* On the foundation of *The
Word of God* is creation, which leads to family values, respect for human
life, right and wrong, good science, and much more. On the foundation
of *The Mind of Man* is evolution, which leads to homosexuality, abortion,
Earth worship, and socialism, among other bad things. It should come
as no surprise that a community linking evolution to all these horrible
consequences would find the evidence for evolution very "unconvincing"
indeed. Creationists respond by arguing, based on their reading of the
Genesis creation accounts, that the earth is only a few thousand years old,
and that each individual species was created separately. Intelligent design
advocates respond by arguing that good science needn't confine itself to
natural explanations, invoking supernatural intervention to explain the
origin of complex biochemical and anatomical structures.

Evangelicals are right that rejection of the supernatural has profound
consequences for morality, and for the status of humans vis-à-vis other

animals (although the consequences are probably not as bad as most evangelicals fear). But they are wrong to equate belief in evolution with a rejection of the supernatural. Although evolution may make it possible to be an intellectually fulfilled atheist, as Richard Dawkins famously quipped, it doesn't make it impossible to be an intellectually fulfilled theist. Why not? Christians may believe that God created life via the evolutionary process, just as they believe God creates a future child in the womb by purely natural means. Christians believe God designed the laws of nature, and there's no reason they can't believe that God designed them in a way that, over the course of evolutionary history, humans would eventually result. Scientific objections to evolution—from both creationist and intelligent design camps—are woefully flawed, and biblical objections even more so.

Creation Science

Neil Shubin, a paleontologist at the University of Chicago, was flipping through a geology textbook one day when he saw a picture that caught his eye: an exposed rock face from Ellesmere Island, at the tip of Canada. Dating evidence placed the rocks squarely in the Devonian period, about 375 million years back. This was thought to be a crucial period in evolutionary history. About 15 million years earlier, paleontologists looking for vertebrates had only found fish; about 15 million years later, 360 million years back, they found both fish and amphibians. Shubin realized that Ellesmere Island held fresh water at the time. If there were any transition fossils between lobe-finned fish and amphibians—both of which inhabited fresh water—this would be both the place and time to look. So in 1999, Shubin gathered up his team and headed for the tip of Canada.

After repeated trips between the island and Chicago, from 1999 to 2005, "we hit the jackpot," Shubin states. The team found the remains of a creature with both gills for breathing in water and lungs with a rib cage for breathing out of it, with scales like a fish but two eyes resting atop an amphibian-like, flat head. Moreover, although the creature's hind limbs were simple fins, its front limbs had sturdy bones that would have enabled it to push its head and neck out of a stream and graze on vegetation surrounding its banks. Shubin named the find *Tiktaalik roseae* and published his findings in *Nature* in 2006.

Creationists have long insisted, in accord with their reading of the Genesis phrase "after their kind," that immutable forms of animal exist outside of which evolution cannot occur. Sure, bacteria might evolve antibiotic resistance, in this analysis, and the Galapagos finches may have evolved different beaks to suit unique dietary habits. But bacteria don't evolve into birds. Evolution may occur within predefined categories— and there is a branch of creation science dedicated to elucidating such categories, called baraminology—but it does not occur between them. In this analysis, fossils like *Tiktaalik* shouldn't exist.

But they do exist. And *Tiktaalik roseae* is not the only fossil that challenges the baraminologist scheme. Shortly after Darwin's *Origin of Species* was published in 1859, the remains of a creature later called *Archaeopteryx* were found, sporting a reptilian's bony tail and teeth but also a bird's feathered wings. Over the last several decades, a fossil series connecting land mammals and water mammals has been uncovered, from the semiaquatic *Pakicetus*, to the sea-lion-like *Ambulocetus*, to the exclusively water-dwelling *Dorudon*, whose two-foot-long hind limbs trailed along uselessly as its fifty-foot body glided through the water.

Probably the most powerful challenge to creationism comes from modern genetics: Genetic research has revealed that organisms still carry many genes from their evolutionary ancestors. Birds still carry the genes to make teeth like those of their reptile ancestors, and the teeth can be expressed in bird tissue by providing the proper stimulus. Genetic information for making hind legs can be found in the whale genome, and it is occasionally turned on; thus, a fraction of whales is regularly born with one or more legs. The same considerations mean that humans are occasionally born with a tail, complete with vertebrae and muscles to control its movement.

Indeed, as the Human Genome Project has revealed, human DNA is littered with broken, nonfunctional genes from proposed evolutionary ancestors. The reason that humans, gorillas, and chimps need to consume vitamin C in their diets—while lower mammals, including primates further down the evolutionary tree, don't—is that humans, gorillas, and chimps all have the same, inactivating mutation in a gene needed to make vitamin C. From an evolutionary perspective, the gene was mutated and rendered nonfunctional in an ape ancestor, then passed on to its evolutionary descendants, including humans. From a creationist perspective, God gave all higher primates the same broken gene for no apparent reason. More than 5 percent of human genes are nonfunctional. Many of these are also nonfunctional in apes but functional in lower vertebrates.

During my undergraduate days at Calvin College, a symposium was held on the origin of life. After detailing his research, a creation scientist from the Center for Origins Research ended with a shockingly candid statement: Creation science is not a viable scientific alternative to evolutionary science. He acknowledged that the data just aren't there and that creationist explanations are not adequate at all. "But you know what?" he continued. "I'd rather stand before Jesus someday and say, 'Well, maybe I took you too seriously,' than, 'Maybe I didn't take you seriously enough.'" This bright young creationist, with a PhD in biochemistry from the University of Virginia, was more than willing to endure a lifetime of scorn and mockery in order to stand up for God's Word when the secular world and liberal Christians were turning away from it. Like many scientists from fundamentalist and evangelical homes, he had chosen to devote his entire career to creation science because he believed the Bible says so and the Bible is true. Creationist Henry Morris explains this mentality best when he writes, "The main reason for insisting on the universal Flood as a fact of history and as the primary vehicle for geological interpretation is that God's Word plainly teaches it! No geological difficulties, real or imagined, can be allowed to take precedence over the clear statements and necessary inferences of Scripture." Creationism is not ultimately about science; it's about the Bible.

That alone doesn't make it invalid (what ultimately makes a scientific theory invalid is not where it comes from—whether it be the Bible or some other source—but whether it can offer a coherent explanation of relevant data). But it does mean that no amount of scientific evidence will be enough to convince Christians to abandon creation science, in all its manifestations, as long as they believe that this is what the Bible says.

The Creation of Creationism

As it turns out, the strongest argument against the creationist reading of scripture comes from creationists themselves. As we saw in Chapter 3, in the 1970s, creationists largely abandoned the idea that theirs was the only viable interpretation of the science. Instead, they argued that their interpretation was simply the result of approaching the data from a "biblical" perspective. Thus, creationists began arguing that schools should teach both sides—creation science and evolution science—as two paradigm-relative interpretations of the data. At the same time, they began to abandon Bacon's understanding of science in favor of the philosophy articulated by Abraham Kuyper and Thomas Kuhn. Whereas Bacon had argued that true science only occurs when one approaches the data without any presuppositions, Kuyper and Kuhn argued that one cannot interpret data without presuppositions. In their analysis, scientific data are always inescapably interpreted within a framework of assumptions, a "paradigm," as Kuhn put it.

And this is where creationism runs into problems. When creationists adopted Kuhn's understanding of interpretation in the 1970s (applying it to science), they retained Bacon's (contradictory) understanding of interpretation (applying it to the Bible). Hence, they now argue based on an interpretation of the Bible they deem self-evident and objective that the scientific data can be reconciled with young earth creationism because interpretation is not self-evident and objective. As one creationist wrote in the 1970s, "The widely accepted concept of the complete objectivity of the individual scientist is naïve—an unfortunate twentieth century myth." One of the main arguments of this book is that the widely accepted concept of the complete objectivity of the biblical interpreter is also naive—an unfortunate nineteenth-century myth.

Creationism fails, even by its own standards, because creationists are not ultimately defending the Bible. Indeed, they cannot do so even in principle, any more than, on Kuhn's analysis, a scientist can simply defend "nature," construed independently of a paradigm. They can only defend a paradigm-relative interpretation of the Bible. And that is precisely what they do. The best way to see this is to examine creationism in light of history, looking at the contingent assumptions that were gradually assembled—one by one over the course of recent history—to make the creationist approach to the Bible possible. In the process, we will see that creationism did not fall in a pristine package from the hand of God or flow from a pure, disinterested, innocent reading of the Bible; it was created by humans at a specific time in history as a consequence of a number of historical factors.

THE TWO BOOKS

"The proposition that the Bible must be interpreted by science is all but self-evident," wrote evangelical theologian Charles Hodge in 1859. "Nature is as truly a revelation of God as the Bible; and we only interpret the Word of God by the Word of God when we interpret the Bible by science." Hodge, a professor of theology at Princeton Theological Seminary, is widely considered one of the fathers of modern evangelical theology (and was one of the major defenders of the doctrine of the inerrancy of scripture in his time); his books on theology were required reading in evangelical seminaries for much of the twentieth century. Nineteenth-century evangelicals, such as Hodge, placed a high premium on science precisely *because* they believed God created the natural world; learning about nature was learning about God's creation, which in turn, was learning about God. Both the Bible and nature were seen as two different books written by the same author, and one could not truly understand the Bible without understanding the natural world as well.

This "two books doctrine," as it has been called, has been a staple feature of Christianity and served as a rationale for paying close attention to the best science of the day. "We know [God] in two manners," wrote the authors of the Belgic Confession in 1512. "First, by the creation, preservation and government of the universe, which is before our eyes as a most beautiful book. . . . Second . . . by his holy and divine Word; that is to say, as far as is necessary for us to know in this life." The conviction behind the "two books doctrine"—that to understand the world, Christians must pay attention to both the Bible and science, allowing science to guide the interpretation of the Bible when necessary—is usefully contrasted with what might be called the "one book doctrine" behind creationism: that the only source of true knowledge about God is the Bible. As creationist Henry Morris puts it, in an essay titled "The Bible *Is* a Textbook of Science," "[I]f man wishes to know anything at all about Creation . . . his sole source of true information is that of divine revelation. . . . This is our textbook on the science of Creation!" Likewise, John Morris writes that Christians should not "be looking to scientific opinion to interpret the Bible for us—the Bible will interpret itself. We just need to believe it."

The two books doctrine flows from another conviction (and here, we begin a journey from premodern Christianity to the present): that the interpretation of scripture is guided by assumptions, theology, and a portrait of the empirical world. The early Christians strongly sensed that the meaning of the Bible was not self-evident because many detractors from the church also based their positions on the Bible. For every verse theologians like Augustine could cite in support of newly emerging "orthodox" doctrine, heretics could cite one back. The Bible was used to support a wide variety of positions, with different communities simply emphasizing different passages, interpreting words this way instead of that, and generally, reading the Bible in a way that supported their unique theological convictions. So the early Christian theologians decided that sound interpretations of the Bible must not only draw on biblical passages (since even heretical doctrines can be justified doing that); they must also be consistent with church instruction on such issues as the deity of Jesus, the triune nature of God, and the purpose of the law. This guide for interpretation was called the "Rule of Faith," and was justified with respect to both the Bible and also the newly developing theology of the Church. The Rule of Faith was not an independent tradition to be held up next to "what the Bible says"; rather, it was a theological framework that guided Christians in deciding "what the Bible says" in the first place.

There were several theological notions contained in the Rule of Faith that allowed Christians to reconcile new scientific discoveries with their understanding of the Bible. One of them was the doctrine of "divine accommodation." This doctrine, found in Augustine but articulated most clearly by the Protestant John Calvin (writing in the 1600s), held that because God is infinitely great and above humans, God must condescend to communicate with them, speaking to them like a parent speaks to a child. As Augustine put it, "The narrative of the inspired writer brings the matter down to the capacity of children." Or as John Calvin put it, speaking of Genesis, "Moses wrote in a popular style things which, without instruction, all ordinary persons endued with common sense, are able to understand; but astronomers investigate with great labour whatever the sagacity of the human mind can comprehend."

The doctrine of divine accommodation was used to explain why the Bible contains statements that reflect ancient, outdated ideas about the natural world. The Bible was first given to people who held ancient, outdated ideas about the natural world. When they looked up at the sky, they saw a solid dome with lights in it. When they looked around them, they saw a flat earth. The Bible speaks their language because God condescended to their view of the world in order to be intelligible to them. Calvin notes, for example, that the Bible speaks of "the two great luminaries" in the sky, referring to the sun and the moon. But during the time Calvin lived, astronomers believed the two great luminaries in the sky were the sun and the planet Saturn. Calvin explains this apparent inconsistency by noting that, even though astronomers during his period might see the sun and Saturn as the "two great luminaries," to an ancient person looking up at the sky, the sun and the moon appear to be the two biggest lights. Thus, the Bible refers to these planets in a way that ancient people would understand. God condescends to communicate with humans.

ALLEGORY

Another aspect of biblical interpretation that reduced the prospect of Bible-science conflicts was the prevalence of allegorical interpretation. In the premodern world, allegorical interpretations were fanciful readings that illustrated orthodox theological and moral ideas accepted on other grounds. Each passage of the Bible could usually be subject to both a literal and an allegorical interpretation—and both were prevalent before the Reformation, with the Antiochene school favoring literalism and the Alexandrian school allegory—but if the literal sense of a passage would offend Christian belief or morals or otherwise put the truth of scripture in question (by producing conflicts with science, for example), then the passage must be interpreted allegorically. As Augustine put it, "[A]nything in the divine discourse that cannot be related either to good morals or to the true faith should be taken as figurative." Allegorical interpretation thus provided a purpose for portions of the Bible that were too bizarre or offensive for interpreters when taken literally; interpreted allegorically, those portions of the Bible communicated deeper theological truths.

In his allegorical interpretation of Genesis, for example, Augustine interprets the "days" of creation as referring, variously, to scripture, angels, and Christian baptism. The first two verses of Genesis read: "In the beginning, when God created the heavens and the earth, the earth was a formless void and darkness covered the face of the deep, while a wind from God swept over the face of the waters." Augustine finds a reference to the Trinity in these verses, reading the "wind from God" as a reference to the Holy Spirit and "in the beginning" as a reference to Jesus, who, according to John 1:1, "was with God [the Father] in the beginning."

Augustine ends this exposition, in an affront to modern evangelical sensibilities, by pondering the wide number of possible interpretations of Genesis—and condemning the tendency to advance only one to the exclusion of others.

> Since, then, so rich a variety of highly plausible
> interpretations can be culled from those words,
> consider how foolish it is rashly to assert that Moses
> intended one particular meaning rather than any of the
> others. If we engage in hurtful strife as we attempt to
> expound his words, we offend against the very charity
> for the sake of which he said all those things.

Indeed, not only does Augustine welcome multiple interpretations of Genesis, recognizing that many different interpretations may be consistent with the Rule of Faith and the best science of the day; he insists on multiple interpretations, seeing them as commanded with the injunction to "increase and multiply." Augustine writes:

> Observe that scripture offers us a single truth,
> couched in simple words, when it tells us, "In the
> beginning God created heaven and earth." But is it not
> interpreted in manifold ways? Leaving aside fallacious
> and mistaken theories, are there not divergent schools
> of true opinion? This corresponds to the increase and
> multiplication of human progeny.

Whereas Genesis 1 is a site of infighting and exclusion for many evangelicals, for Augustine, it provided an opportunity to marvel at the variety of meanings that may legitimately be assigned to scripture.

THE BIBLE AS SCIENCE TEXTBOOK

Things changed with the Protestant Reformation in the 1500s. Celebrating interpretive diversity is nice when Christians generally agree on core aspects of the faith, but when they do not agree, and a desire arises to prove one side is right and the other wrong, a bit more certainty about the validity of one's interpretation is required. Protestants found the certainty they needed to challenge the Catholic Church by minimizing allegory—which was far too playful and unpredictable for their purposes—and privileging literal interpretations. This shift had a significant impact on Bible-science relationships. Oxford's Peter Harrison explains, in his landmark historical book, *The Bible, Protestantism, and the Rise of Natural Science*:

> With the new biblical literalism which followed the
> reformation, many portions of scripture were read
> for the first time as having, as their primary sense,
> history. . . . Whereas the accounts of creation in the
> book of Genesis had previously provided scope for

the imaginations of exegetes given to allegory, now
the significance of these stories was seen to lie in their
literal truth as depicting past events.

Many past Christians, for example, had interpreted the story of Noah's flood as an allegory for the Church. In the story, Noah builds a large boat to save himself and his family—representing Christians—from a worldwide flood God sends in judgment of the rest of the world—non-Christians. But "for the more worldly . . . seventeenth-century reader," Harrison explains, "these narratives came to have present significance because they provoked scientific and cosmological questions, or provided knowledge which could be categorised as 'science.'" Questions shifted from the potential theological significance of various details of the story to "more mundane questions of science and logistics. Where did the waters come from and where did they eventually go?"

This new view of the Bible as a major source of factual information about nature and history had a profound impact on Christian understanding of what was so special about "scripture." Whereas previously, much of the magic of scripture lay in its hidden allegorical meanings, now scripture became a lot like other books—another source of factual information. Since the magic of scripture could no longer be found in its multiple meanings, it was relocated. Scripture may be another source of facts about nature and the past, but its uniqueness came to lie in the supposition that it provides much more accurate facts about nature and the past than other books. Harrison notes:

> The Bible thus came to compete with secular writings
> on their own ground. . . . Where the Bible was
> not obviously—that is at a literal level—conveying
> theological or moral information, it was thought to
> provide knowledge relating to history and geography,
> or the arts and sciences. Indeed, allegory [was] now

regarded as having for centuries blinded readers to
the history and science which could be found in the
scriptures.

One theologian at the time noted that Christians would have figured out where the Garden of Eden was by then but for "the negligence
of former times, in not making out the truth of it by the help of Ge-
ography, but blanching it over with Allegorical or impertinent and ridiculous interpretations." Many intellectuals, in an age obsessed with
science, began to argue that the Bible also contained modern scientific
theories. One Cambridge University professor, for example, claimed to
find biblical sanction for the corpuscular theory of matter, Descartes's
theory of planetary motion, and a heliocentric solar system (all but one
of those theories have since been abandoned). "[T]hose truths were
ever lodged in the tent of Moses," he wrote, "though men have not had,
for these many Ages, the leisure or opportunity of unlocking them till
now."

It was in this context that the flood of Noah first began to be widely
interpreted as a means of explaining the fossil record, and the book of
Genesis as providing a specific age for the earth. Indeed, the creationist
approach to the Bible is very much a part of this tradition. Henry Morris,
speaking of the Bible, writes of "the great number of scientific truths that
have lain hidden within its pages for thirty centuries or more, only to
be discovered by man's enterprise within the last few centuries or even
years." And in an age in which "science" was the ultimate arbiter of truth,
confirming supposed biblical claims about history and natural processes
functioned as confirmation of Christianity.

ELLEN G. WHITE

Of course, there was a flip side to this equation. If science could confirm empirical claims made by biblical interpretations, it could also re-

fute them. And the new nineteenth-century science of geology began to do just that. Shortly after the age of science produced interpretations of the Bible teaching a young earth and worldwide flood that explained the fossil record (in the sixteenth through eighteenth centuries), it then produced scientific data suggesting an old earth and that a worldwide flood had never occurred (in the nineteenth century). Christians at the time had little problem acknowledging these new discoveries. Drawing on the two books doctrine, one evangelical reasoned, "If both records are from God, there can be no real contradiction between them." America's top geologists, who were mostly evangelical Christians at the time, began to embrace the idea that the earth was very old and that a geologically significant flood had never occurred, construing the Genesis "days" as "long periods of time" or embracing the "gap theory" that an indefinitely long period of time passed between the first two verses of Genesis.

There were some detractors from this reinterpretation. Foreshadowing the modern creationist movement, the "scriptural geologists," as they were called, believed in a short history for the earth and a worldwide flood. In the 1820s, these authors—all popular writers with no formal training in geology or biblical studies—began publishing polemics against the new interpretations of Genesis, calling their advocates "wholly at war with the Bible." The interpretations of the new geology, they noted, involved assumptions.

One of the scriptural geologists was a woman by the name of Ellen Gould White. White believed God had revealed to her what happened during the flood of Genesis and published her views on the matter in 1864. She claimed God showed her how the flood had destroyed animal and plant life, forming the fossil record. She also argued that the earth is young and the "days" of Genesis *must* be interpreted as twenty-four-hour periods of time. White was a founder of Seventh-day Adventistism—which claims that the Christian day of rest should be Saturday, not Sunday—and thus, had unique reasons for protesting a reinterpretation of

the Genesis days. As historian Ronald Numbers explains, the reinterpretation "struck at the very basis of the Sabbath—and the identity of Seventh-day
Adventists—by suggesting that the seventh day of creation had not been a
literal 24-hour period." White's writing is held at the same level as scripture by Seventh-day Adventists, who believe God did indeed inspire her.
It is also the origin of the creationist interpretation of the Bible.

EVANGELICAL EVOLUTIONISTS

Nevertheless, nearly a hundred years would pass before White's interpretation of Genesis would be disseminated to and widely embraced
by evangelicals as "the biblical view." Indeed, the writing of the scriptural geologists was not taken seriously by mainstream evangelicals at
the time. Whereas the thought of evangelicals is largely dominated by
popular leaders today, in the 1800s, academics and intellectuals played
a much larger role. And thus, evangelical Christians at the time did not
have much of a problem accepting the idea that the earth is old and that a
worldwide flood never occurred. This shift was so thorough, that, as one
author notes, "During the early years of the twentieth century there were
virtually no visible Christian advocates of a young earth, or a geologically
important flood . . . or of the necessity of taking Genesis as teaching any
such doctrines." The new biblical interpretations forged by mainstream,
evangelical Christian geologists and theologians became "the bedrock of
orthodoxy for nineteenth-century American evangelicalism."

Thus, when Darwin's *Origin of Species* was published in 1857, few saw
it as a major threat to either the Bible or Christianity. B. B. Warfield—an
evangelical theologian operating out of Princeton Theological Seminary,
who was a major proponent of the doctrine of the inerrancy of scripture
that is championed by contemporary creationists (Henry Morris cites
Warfield as the source of his understanding of the doctrine in *The Genesis
Flood*)—wrote in 1888: "I do not think that there is any general statement in the Bible or any part of the account of creation, either as given

in Gen. I&II or elsewhere alluded to, that need be opposed to evolution." Warfield, in fact, found the theory of evolution could fit quite neatly with his Calvinism. A John Calvin familiar with modern science, he suggested, "would have been a precursor of the modern evolutionary theorists . . . for he teaches, as they teach, the modification of the original world-stuff into the varied forms which constitute the ordered world, by the instrumentality of secondary causes." He continued: "Calvin's doctrine of creation is, if we have understood it aright . . . an evolutionary one."

Another evangelical theologian at Princeton—Charles Hodge—had more reservations. Like most other evangelicals at the time, however, his reservations were not based on the Bible but his sense that evolution posed a threat to William Paley's argument from design. Nevertheless, while he called Darwinism "atheism," he also wrote, "A man . . . may be an evolutionist without being a Darwinian." Accepting the theory of evolution, he noted, does not preclude belief in God: "there is a theistic and an atheistic form of the nebular hypothesis as to the origin of the universe; so there may be a theistic interpretation of the Darwinian theory."

This general agreement—that the theory of evolution could be reconciled with orthodox Christianity—waned only slightly with the rise of Christian fundamentalism in the early 1900s (before being completely obliterated in the 1920s). The fundamentalist movement arose out of widespread anxiety over modern challenges to Christian belief. Universities, once ruled by evangelical doctrine, gradually began jettisoning supernatural beliefs around the turn of century. German higher criticism questioned the accuracy of the Bible. Theological liberalism was infiltrating mainstream churches. In response to these challenges, evangelical leaders produced *The Fundamentals*, a collection of essays setting forth what they viewed as the essential doctrines of Christianity. The essays, published from 1910 to 1915, featured articles from a wide range of scholars. Three million copies were distributed to evangelicals across the United States, and the collection became the founding document of the Christian fundamentalist movement. Four contributors to *The Fundamentals* wrote articles on evolution. Two of them supported it.

George Frederick Wright, a theologian and geologist from Oberlin College, wrote the longest article on evolution for *The Fundamentals*. In his essay, "Some Analogies between Calvinism and Darwinism," he called evolutionary theory "the Calvinistic interpretation of nature." A second contributor to *The Fundamentals*, a theology professor from Glasgow named James Orr, generally agreed. "Assume God—as many devout evolutionists do—to be immanent in the evolutionary process, and His intelligence and purpose to be expressed in it; then evolution, so far from conflicting with theism, may become a new and heightened form of the theistic argument."

Two other authors, both lesser known, issued vitriolic attacks on evolution, foreshadowing the coming shift in evangelicalism from nuanced, scholarly engagement to reactionary, populist thought. Evolution-believing Christians, the first author suggested, were "of low moral quality." In line with the strategies of the later creationist movement, the author masked his theological unease behind scientific objections, collecting quotations from scientists to suggest that evolution was poorly supported by the facts. The second contributor, Reverend Henry Beach, deemed evolution "immoral" and "ridiculous." His main two objections were that evolution is only a theory, not a fact, and in any case, it is too morally offensive to be taken seriously.

The Rise of Evangelical Antievolutionists

While the early fundamentalist movement embraced a wide range of views on evolution, during the 1920s antievolutionism became a boundary marker for distinguishing Christian insiders from non-Christian outsiders. World War I exacerbated the sense of cultural change and secularization that had earlier led to the production of *The Fundamentals*.

Anti-German propaganda regularly linked Germany with higher criticism, which suggested the Bible was full of historical inaccuracies, and the perception spread that Germany's cultural decline was a consequence of the acceptance of social Darwinism and evolution in general. Challenges to the faith abounded in America as well. Universities were becoming increasingly secular. College students were abandoning Christianity in unprecedented numbers. This sense of cultural change was most profound in the South, which had lost the Civil War and perceived the abolition of slavery as resulting from a liberal approach to the Bible. Southerners, who had championed the "plain sense" of specific biblical texts to defend slavery, were not about to embrace allegorical or theologically nuanced readings of the first chapters of Genesis. Thus, Southern states passed the first laws against the teaching of evolution.

Importantly, evangelical thought was dominated by the understanding of interpretation articulated by Bacon. What were the implications of this approach to the Bible? Notre Dame historian George Marsden explains what this meant to evangelicals at the time: "The Bible, according to the democratic popularization of this view, is best interpreted by the naïve readings that common people today give it." Thus, in the words of one early fundamentalist, "In ninety-nine out of a hundred cases, the meaning that the plain man gets out of the Bible is the correct one." This idea—that some people approach the Bible objectively whereas others bring all sorts of "biases," "assumptions," "agendas" and the like—continues to guide the thought of lay evangelicals today, as we've seen.

This mind-set is well illustrated by a cartoon from a young earth creationist book. "There are various ways to understand Genesis," a white-haired professor, representing the academic elite, declares, pointing to a board with the words "Gap Theory," "Theistic Evolution," and "Progressive Creation." In the next frame, an incredulous student stands up—representing the common man—and champions his own unbiased reading of the text: "Professor, why can't I just believe what the Bible says?" The idea is that whereas some people, usually the "common man," simply accept "what the Bible says," others, often the educated "elite," introduce all sorts of "biases," "agendas," or "interpretations."

Nevertheless, despite the conviction of many that young earth creationism self-evidently flows from a plain, unbiased approach to the biblical text, nearly all of the first evangelical antievolutionists—themselves, champions of a plain, unbiased approach to scripture—did not believe in a young earth, or a geologically significant flood. Many of them, including William Jennings Bryan and several editors of *The Fundamentals*, accepted a modified form of the evolutionary hypothesis. R. A. Torrey, a chief editor of *The Fundamentals*, for example, declared, "Anyone who is at all familiar with the Bible . . . knows that the use of the word 'day' is not limited to periods of twenty-four hours. It is frequently used of a period of time of an entirely undefined length," adding that he could happily accept evolution if the evidence became strong enough. Another popular strategy was to suggest that an indefinite period of time passed between the first two verses of Genesis (the so-called gap theory). Indeed, this interpretation became so popular among fundamentalists that one young earth creationist at the time complained that it had become "a Fundamentalist dogma; and when I say dogma in that connection I mean DOGMA and then some. . . . The thing is an obsession."

Indeed, it turns out that, for most of the first half of the twentieth century, Seventh-day Adventists comprised the only significant number of adherents to the idea of a worldwide flood responsible for the fossil record and a young earth. Adventists championed these ideas because as we've seen earlier, the founder of their group, the nineteenth-century prophetess Ellen G. White, claimed in her writing—believed by Adventists to be inspired by God—that she had been shown a vision of the events. One of White's disciples was a man by the name of George McCready Price. Price, who had no formal training in either science or theology, believed White's vision was indeed divinely inspired and dedicated his life to finding scientific support for it. Price's biggest contribution to the antievolution cause was his 1923 book, *The New Geology*, in which he attacked a central piece of evidence for evolution—the succession of species in the fossil record—by arguing, alternatively, that there was no general order to the fossil record, and that, in any case, any order that did exist could be explained by a worldwide flood. Price's views were almost universally accepted by fellow Seventh-day Adventists, but they were viewed with suspicion by fundamentalists, who were uneasy about the denomination's veneration of the writings of Ellen G. White.

Price's views had little impact on evangelical and fundamentalist Christianity until the 1960s, when Henry Morris and John Whitcomb appropriated and popularized them in their 1961 book, *The Genesis Flood*. Henry Morris, a Southern Baptist with a PhD in hydraulic engineering, believed the Genesis "days" could only be interpreted as twenty-four-hour periods. He had a hard time reconciling his position with science, however, until he encountered *The New Geology*, by Price. Morris was so enamored with Price's interpretation of both science and the Bible that he teamed up with Whitcomb, a theologian at Grace Theological Seminary, to write *The Genesis Flood*, a revision and updating of Price. Evangelicals and fundamentalists bought the book in droves. Ellen G. White's divinely inspired interpretation of Genesis, filtered through Price, then filtered through Morris, was widely disseminated to the evangelical community, and for the first time, as historian Ronald Numbers remarks, "fundamentalists in large numbers began to read Genesis in the Pricean manner and to equate his views with the intended message of Moses."

The dissemination of young earth creationism was furthered by the rise of the evangelical Right in the late 1970s and the concomitant resurgence of antievolution political advocacy. The proponents of creationism argued that schools should "teach both sides": "creation science" and "evolution science." "Creation science" was defined as the "young earth creationism" formulated by Price. In a twist of irony, schools were now being urged to teach a form of creationism that most evangelicals and fundamentalists had rejected only thirty years earlier. The main argument for "teaching both sides" was that, in line with the philosophy of Thomas Kuhn, interpretation always occurs within a framework of assumptions, a "paradigm," as Kuhn put it. The new young earth creationists were simply interpreting the data within "the biblical paradigm."

Creationists, and evangelicals in general, establish an opposition between God's Word and human ideas—or, as it is often put, between the "words of God" and the "words of Man"—suggesting that their own beliefs are grounded squarely on the words of God while those of scientists are founded on the rather flimsy, shifting foundation of the words of Man. But what the above history demonstrates is that the way creationists construe the "Word of God" is determined by "words of Man" (and words of Woman, in this case). Mark Noll puts it best when he notes that "millions of evangelicals think they are defending the Bible by defending creation science, but in reality they are giving ultimate authority to the merely temporal, situated, and contextualized interpretations of the Bible that arose from the mania for science of the early nineteenth century." Like evangelicals who think the Bible says life begins at conception, like profamily activists who believe excluding gays from marriage is ultimately defending the Bible, and even like progressives who think advocating "environmental stewardship" is a mere reflection of "the biblical view," creationists are not ultimately defending the Bible. They are defending the very human set of assumptions, cultural values, and interests they bring to it. In the process, they both depart from the theological beliefs that guided past Christian interpretation of scripture and mask the assumptions that guide their own interpretation.

Sky Dome

An additional problem for the creationist approach to the Bible—aside from the fact that it is based on a grid of historically contingent assumptions that were not shared by many Christians in the past—is that creationists do not employ their own interpretive principles in a consistent fashion. Creationists Henry Morris and John Morris, for example, rely on the modern method of constructing the ancient context in which a text was written to suggest how the original audience would likely have understood Genesis. "I hold to a historical grammatical hermeneutic which seeks to discern the actual meaning the author was communicating to the reader," John Morris explains. Morris points out that the original readers of Genesis almost certainly would have understood the word "day" as referring to a twenty-four-hour period of time. And many serious biblical scholars concede his point.

So what's the problem? Creationists are simply defending what the text meant to its original audience, right? Not quite. While the original audience probably would have understood Genesis as affirming a creation in six, twenty-four-hour days, they also would have understood Genesis, and the entire Old Testament, for that matter, as affirming their ancient cosmology. Like their neighbors, ancient Israelites did not understand the physical makeup of the universe as we do today. When they looked up at the sky, they did not see an infinite expanse of outer space, filled with galaxies, stars, and planets; like their ancient Near Eastern neighbors in Babylon and Egypt, they saw a solid dome with lights in it. Beyond and beneath that dome were "the waters," kept precariously at bay by the solid dome. Every once in a while, the windows in the ceiling of the dome opened, as did the so-called fountains of the deep, letting water pour in to irrigate what they believed was a flat earth resting on pillars (sitting directly above "sheol," the realm of the dead).

The Old Testament preserves this ancient understanding of the universe. Thus, in Genesis 1:6–8, we read, "And God said, 'Let there be a dome in the midst of the waters, and let it separate the waters from the waters.' So God made the dome and separated the waters that were under the dome from the waters that were above the dome. And it was so.

God called the dome Sky." "Can you join him in spreading out the skies," Job 37:18 asks, which is "hard as a mirror of cast bronze?" As to the water above the sky dome, we read in Psalm 148:4, "Praise him, you highest heavens, and you waters above the heavens!" And when the flood of Noah occurred, a central event in the creationist scheme, "the windows of the heavens were opened" (Genesis 7:11). The windows in the sky dome opened and closed at other times as well, such as when the flood of Noah ended (Genesis 8:2, "the windows of the heavens were closed, the rain from the heavens was restrained") or when the Israelites obeyed God (Malachi 3:10, "See if I will not open the windows of heaven for you and pour down for you an overflow of blessing"). And this is to say nothing of the pillars supporting the earth: "The pillars of the earth are the Lord's," 1 Samuel 2:8 affirms, "and on them he has set the world" (see also 2 Samuel 22:16, Psalms 75:3 and 104:5, and Job 9:6 and 38:4). It is also to say nothing of sheol, the realm of the dead directly beneath the earth. As Isaiah 14:9 has it, "Sheol beneath is stirred up to meet you when you come . . . it raises from their thrones all who were kings of the nations" (see also Genesis 37:35, Deuteronomy 32:22, and Job 26:6).

Needless to say, creationists do not go nearly far enough, even by their own standards. If they wish to equate the ancient audience's understanding of the Bible with the meaning of the biblical text—to "take Genesis seriously," as they put it—they've got their work cut out for them. They must not only argue that the world is young, that each species was created separately, and that a universal flood occurred; they must also argue that we live under a solid dome in a universe filled with water, on a flat earth supported by pillars. Creationists, of course, do not wish to do this, and thus, interpret these parts of the Bible by drawing on modern scientific knowledge. Henry Morris, for example, draws on knowledge of modern science to suggest that the "firmament" of Genesis—which would have been understood by the ancient Israelites as referring to the sky dome—should be understood as referring to the "atmosphere," an entity characterized only in the past few centuries. Creationists are here allowing modern science—the "words of man"—to shape their understanding of the Word of God. And if they're willing to do it when it comes to the firmament, why not when it comes to the age of the earth or the origin of species? As evangelical theologian Charles Hodge wrote in 1853, "When the Bible speaks of the foundations, or of the pillars of the earth, or of the solid heavens, or of the motion of the sun, do not you and every other sane man, interpret this language by the facts of science? For five thousand years the Church understood the Bible to teach that the earth stood still in space, and that the sun and stars revolved around it. Science has demonstrated that this is not true. Shall we go on to interpret the Bible so as to make it teach the falsehood that the sun moves around the earth, or shall we interpret it by science, and make the two harmonize?" Although creationists may assert that the Bible is a scientific textbook, they fail to apply that assessment consistently.

What happens when we approach Genesis without expecting a treatise on modern science? What happens when we approach it with different assumptions, in a different interpretive paradigm? One of the first things to notice is that the cosmology assumed in Genesis and the Old Testament—flat earth, sky dome, pillars, and the like—was not uniquely held by the ancient Israelites. This is how ancient people, in general, viewed the universe. A helpful way of interpreting Genesis is to approach it, as theologian Karl Barth recommended, "with the ears of an ancient Egyptian."

Ancient people not only lived on a flat earth, supported by pillars, under a sky dome; they also lived in a world where humans were created as slaves to the gods, the sun was divine, and matter eternal. One take on Genesis is that it is not so much interested in correcting the ancients' understanding of the physical world as it is in changing their theological understanding of it. Humans are not slaves to the gods, but the crown of creation, made in God's image; the sun is not divine, but almost an afterthought, created on day four; and matter is not necessary and eternal but created and wholly dependent on God. Genesis told ancients, in short, that their sky dome was created by God. Reclaiming the doctrine of divine accommodation, Genesis can be seen as an instance of God condescending to the physical worldview of the ancients in order to transform their theological worldview. God is even presented in human terms, as a worker who turns on a light on day one before going about the rest of God's work during the remaining days. Indeed, when the God of Genesis is understood as a worker, God's actions become a model for our own: work for six days then rest on the seventh. From this perspective, Genesis serves both to show humans they should rest on the Sabbath and to challenge the theology of ancient pagans.

Intelligent Design

The Supreme Court banned creationism from public schools in 1987. Creationism is religion, not science, they argued, and therefore, teaching it would violate the establishment clause of the First Amendment. That same year, creationists changed strategy, shifting their rhetoric from appeals to a "creator" to appeals to an "intelligent designer." Immediately after the Supreme Court decision, the editors of the leading creationist textbook, *Of Pandas and People*, responded by using a global word processor to take the word "creator" out of the textbook and put "designer" in its place. In the famous Dover trial in 2005 on the constitutionality of intelligent design, John E. Jones, a district judge in Pennsylvania who was appointed by George W. Bush, decried the strategy as "a purposeful change of words . . . effected without any corresponding change in content." The evolution of creationism, apparently, was not substantial enough for Judge Jones. He ruled against intelligent design.

To be fair, however, intelligent design is not the same as creationism, even if its motivating concerns are similar. Whereas creationism primarily attacks the thesis of common ancestry, the idea that all biological life descended by natural means from a common ancestor, intelligent design attacks the theory of natural selection, a postulated mechanism to explain how descent from a common ancestor occurred. Indeed, even many leading proponents of intelligent design, including Michael Behe, accept the proposition that humans evolved from primates. They just don't think *all* evolution can be explained by natural means.

Natural selection is the main mechanism thought to drive evolution. Whereas the thesis of common ancestry simply states *that* all biological life evolved from a common ancestor, the theory of natural selection postulates *how* evolution occurred. The theory of natural selection flows from the observation that the organisms within a particular species come in many different varieties and that, in a given environment, some of those varieties are more likely to survive than others. A given species of bacteria, for example, will contain individual bacteria carrying different versions of many genes. If we put these bacteria in a solution containing antibiotics, only those carrying antibiotic-resistance genes will survive, passing on those genes to descendants. Eventually, bacteria carrying the resistant gene will be the only ones left. This means that physicians must use new antibiotics each year to wage war on the bacteria that have evolved resistance to old ones. Evolutionists say "natural selection at work."

Intelligent design advocates say "not so fast." Noting such examples, leading intelligent design proponent Phillip Johnson argues, in his book *Darwin on Trial*, that "selective change is limited by the inherent variability of the gene pool. . . . It might conceivably be renewed by mutation, but whether (and how often) this happens is not known." Perhaps natural selection doesn't facilitate the creation of new genes but only selects for preexisting ones. Perhaps mutations don't occur, or at least don't occur fast enough to account for the changes we see in the fossil record.

Unfortunately, there's no kind way to say it: Johnson is simply wrong on his facts. Whether (and how often) mutations occur is well known by scientists. In humans, for example, about sixty new mutations occur per generation. Most of these occur outside of genes and have no impact. Most of those occurring within a gene are detrimental, but a small proportion of them are advantageous. Some mutations, for example, have given prostitutes in Africa the ability to resist HIV infection. Mutations that confer a reproductive advantage to organisms will gradually come to predominate in the population. This isn't just an inference from observable data; the process of mutation and natural selection can itself be documented. Brown University cell biologist Kenneth Miller documents several instances of this phenomenon in his book *Only a Theory*. To take one of Miller's examples, consider the following.

Nylon was invented in 1935. As a human-made, entirely new compound, it initially persisted in the natural environment, unable to be digested by microorganisms, which did not have the necessary enzymes to break it down for nutrition. During the 1970s, however, scientists discovered a species of bacteria growing on nylon-rich holding pools. These bacteria had the ability to convert nylon into food thanks to a novel enzyme. Laboratory studies revealed that the enzyme was created by making a second copy of a gene and then introducing a small mutation that allowed the gene's protein product to perform a new action. The initial bacteria with this mutation had an advantage in a pool filled with nylon, and its population exploded. This entire process was duplicated in a controlled laboratory setting, where scientists fed a population of bacteria only nylon. Despite the fact that the bacteria couldn't consume nylon previously, after little more than a week, a group of bacteria emerged that could eat the nylon. Bacteria carrying the mutation had an advantage in their nylon-rich environment and gradually came to predominate as a result.

In response to such evidence, many intelligent design advocates will grant that natural selection can indeed promote the formation of new genes, all the while introducing a distinction between "microevolution" and "macroevolution," characterizing all available evidence as only supporting the possibility of micro changes, not macro ones. This distinction may have had some plausibility two decades ago, when the mechanisms for genetic change were not as well understood and the genomes of different species thought to be quite different from each other, but in light of contemporary scientific knowledge, it can only be viewed as arbitrary and scientifically unfounded. The Human Genome Project has demonstrated that species are different because they have different genomes. And it turns out there isn't much genetic distance between similar species. On a genetic level, for example, humans are 95 percent identical to apes, the difference accounted for by a relatively small number of mutations. Duplicate a few genes there, introduce some point mutations here, eliminate a gene or two there, fuse two chromosomes here, and you've moved from an ape genome to a human genome. The rate of such mutations is well known, and it is more than sufficient to account for even the fastest changes in the fossil record.

Thus, it is unsurprising that one of the only scientifically trained leaders in the intelligent design movement has rejected Johnson's argument and affirmed his belief that humans did, indeed, evolve from apes. That leader is Michael Behe, a biochemist from Lehigh University. Behe's 1996 book, *Darwin's Black Box*, fell like a bombshell on the evangelical community. Suffering from the public defeat of young earth creationism, many evangelicals championed it as a bold new discovery that completely obliterated evolution. "Darwin's Demise," a Biola University magazine proudly announced on its cover: "Something as simple as a mousetrap shows Darwin was wrong." James Dobson took up the new finding in his radio broadcasts, and the evangelical Right, without waiting for additional research or academic discussion, moved quickly to rush this bold new theory into public schools. *Christianity Today* even gave Behe its book-of-the-year award.

What is Behe's argument? Although Behe publicly acknowledges his belief that all biological life, including humans, evolved from a common ancestor, he doesn't think natural selection could have produced every *part* of organisms. In particular, Behe argues, natural selection cannot account for biological structures that are "irreducibly complex." An "irreducibly complex" structure is one that requires all its parts to continue functioning. One example Behe uses is a common mousetrap. A mousetrap has many parts: a platform, a catch (for the cheese), a spring, a hammer (to clamp down on mice unfortunate enough to step on the catch), and a hold-down bar, to keep the hammer ready to strike. All these parts, Behe argues, are required for the mousetrap to function. Take away the hammer, and you have nothing with which to pin down mice; take away the spring, and the hammer can't snap; take away the platform, and there's nothing to hold the rest together.

Since natural selection works via a gradual, step-by-step process, irreducibly complex structures, in Behe's analysis, cannot be developed via natural selection. As Behe explains, "An irreducibly complex system cannot be produced directly by numerous, successive, slight modifications of a precursor system, because *any precursor to an irreducibly complex system that is missing a part is by definition nonfunctional*." The italicized portion of Behe's statement is significant. Natural selection requires that each stage on the way to an adaptation can perform some useful function for its host. You cannot build certain biological structures via natural selection, in this analysis, as you might build a radio, first constructing the circuitry, then creating the casing, then fusing the two, and finally adding an antenna, because you only have a functioning radio at the last stage. You can't listen to songs with a circuit board, and since natural selection only favors structures that give an organism immediate benefit, natural selection, in Behe's analysis, could not favor the formation of irreducibly complex systems (which, according to Behe, only give an organism a benefit when their construction is complete). And Behe argues that organisms are full of irreducibly complex systems. Since these could not have developed via evolution, he argues, they would have to "arise as an integrated unit, in one fell swoop." They must be the product of supernatural intervention by an intelligent designer.

Behe's theory has convinced few scientists. He usually explains this by saying that scientists are biased against the supernatural and will reject any theory that invokes it, no matter how good the theory. One problem with this explanation is that some of the most vocal critics of intelligent design have been theologically conservative Christians, including the Catholic biologist Ken Miller at Brown and the evangelical geneticist Francis Collins. Indeed, the case of intelligent design provides an example of the gap between lay evangelical opinion and scholarly evangelical opinion. Despite the fact that it is virtually considered *the* Christian position on origins among many, if not most, lay evangelicals, and has been eagerly embraced at fundamentalist Bible colleges, the theory receives little support from the biology departments at most leading evangelical colleges. The biology faculty at Calvin College and Gordon College both unanimously reject intelligent design and embrace the idea that God created life through evolution. The American Scientfic Affiliation, a group representing evangelical scholars' thought on science, features widespread acceptance of evolution as well. Even outside evangelicalism, the theory has few proponents among Christian scholars. The Catholic Church, despite its conservative leanings, embraces the theory that God created life through evolution. The reason that leading Christian biologists haven't flocked to intelligent design theory is not because these scientists—who usually have no problem believing Jesus was miraculously raised from the dead—are biased against invoking the supernatural to explain natural phenomena. Indeed, many of these Christian biologists sympathize with intelligent design's critique of naturalism in the sciences and humanities. But they nevertheless reject intelligent design, not because it relies on miracles but because it relies on a scientific argument that is wrong.

The argument for irreducible complexity first makes the correct assumption that a structure in each stage of development must perform some useful function for its host in order to be favored by natural selection. It then makes the incorrect ssumption that the function must be the same at each stage of development. If you want to build a structure that can propel bacteria through liquid, in this analysis, the structure must function to propel bacteria through liquid at each stage of its development. If you want to build a structure that can catch mice, to use Behe's analogy, it must be able to catch mice every step of the way. Behe's argument neglects the fact that the function of structures may change over time as new parts are added. And it assumes that the parts of irreducibly complex structures have no useful function. As Behe states of the mouse-trap, if you take one part away, it is "by definition nonfunctional."

But this is not true of a mousetrap, and it is not true of the other structures Behe labels irreducibly complex either. Taking one part away from a mousetrap may produce a structure that can't catch mice. But it doesn't produce a structure that can't be used for other purposes. It's not difficult to think of alternative possible uses for the small piece of wood that forms the base of a mousetrap, or the giant clip that remains once the catch and hold-down bar are taken away. The same analysis applies to biological structures as well. Indeed, as scientists have shown, even when multiple proteins are removed from a bacterial flagellum, the resulting structure is still useful to its host. The proteins forming the base of a bacterial flagellum, for example, function elsewhere as a membrane channel—a gate allowing molecules to pass in and out of bacterial cells. If protein components are removed from the human bloodclotting system, it can still function, albeit differently, as apparent in lower animals with more simplified clotting systems. The only thing necessary for a structure to evolve is for each stage in its development to be useful. Evolution doesn't require that each predecessor to a structure have the same function. Natural selection favors the combination of parts with different functions to create new structures with new functions.

Aside from the fact that its central scientific argument is flawed, a final major problem for intelligent design is a theological one. It is all well and good to attribute irreducible complexity to the direct agency of God (whom Christians identify as the intelligent designer) when the structures in question are things like the human eye, the mammalian hearing mechanism, or biochemical structures in our cells. But the argument begins to lose some of its luster once we realize that the type of structures Behe describes can be located in the mechanisms that allow the HIV virus to infect immune cells, the biochemical pathways allowing parasites to produce poisons that kill thousands of children in third world countries every day, and in the biochemistry of other pathogens that afflict the human community. According to intelligent design advocates, since such structures are irreducibly complex, they could only be created by the direct, intentional activity of God.

Behe himself, in his 2007 book *The Edge of Evolution*, articulates this implication of his theory without batting an eye:

> Malaria was intentionally designed. The molecular
> machinery with which the parasite invades red blood
> cells is an exquisitely purposeful arrangement of parts.
> C-Eve's children died in her arms partly because an
> intelligent agent deliberately made malaria, or at least
> something very similar to it.

Like it or not, the intelligent design hypothesis takes the problem of evil to a whole new level by requiring us to believe that God not only *allows* the evil that besets humans; God miraculously intervenes in history to facilitate it. If you are looking for the fingerprints of God, in this analysis, you must not only look at the eye, the flagellum, or our own blood-clotting system; you must also look at HIV, malaria, tuberculosis, and other pathogens, all bearing unique, irreducibly complex structures that function only to cause death and destruction in our world. Whereas proponents of theistic evolution may see these as unintentional by-products of the evolutionary process, intelligent design advocates must attribute these to the direct, purposeful, intentional activity of God. Behe's solution to this problem? "Maybe the designer *isn't* all that beneficent or omnipotent." Maybe the designer isn't the Christian God. It is hard to see how any other conclusion is possible if we accept the thesis of irreducible complexity.

Keeping an Open Mind

But shouldn't we keep an open mind? Shouldn't intelligent design be welcomed into colleges and universities in the name of liberty and academic freedom? This was the argument of the 2007 film *Expelled: No Intelligence Allowed*, the latest appeal to the masses by the proponents of intelligent design. The film, hosted by comedian Ben Stein, presents no scientific evidence for intelligent design and no scientific arguments against evolution. Instead, it is all about academic freedom and keeping an open mind—values presumably abandoned by those who have not welcomed intelligent design into universities. Valuing academic freedom, we learn from the film, means treating intelligent design as a worthy opponent of evolutionary theory. The academic merit of intelligent design, which is not discussed in the film, is treated as irrelevant to the question. What the creators of the film failed to recognize is that the same argument could be used to support any position whatsoever—that the Holocaust never occurred, that the moon landing was a government conspiracy, that 9/11 was secretly facilitated by the Bush administration. As philosopher Stanley Fish puts it,

> Polemicists on the right regularly lambaste intellectuals
> on the left for promoting relativism. . . . Whether
> or not this has ever been true of the right's targets,

it is now demonstrably true of the right itself, whose
members now recite the mantras of "teach the
controversy" or "keep the debate open" whenever they
find it convenient. They do so not out of commitment
to scrupulous scholarship . . . but in an effort to
accomplish through misdirection and displacement
what they cannot accomplish through evidence and
argument.

By affirming the value of open-mindedness without placing any restric-
tions on the positions to which universities must be open minded, the
proponents of intelligent design have become proponents of relativism,
asking the academy to accept their theory not because it is a good one but
because rejecting a theory can only result from close-minded dogmatism.

Of course, as with all antievolution advocacy, we should question
whether intelligent-design proponents actually believe in unqualified
open-mindedness or whether this is purely a public relations strategy.
After Nancey Murphy, a philosopher of science at the evangelical Fuller
Theological Seminary, dismissed intelligent design as "so stupid, I don't
want to give them my time," Phillip Johnson, the leader of the intelligent-
design movement and chief architect of its "keep an open mind" strategy,
initiated a campaign to have her fired from the seminary.

A final question we must ask in this chapter is: Who cares? Does it
really matter that, according to a 2005 Pew Research Center poll, "nearly
two-thirds of Americans say that creationism should be taught alongside
evolution in public schools"? Does it really matter that the majority of
Americans support some form of creationism or intelligent design? Does
it really matter that, even among nonscientist Christians with significant
education, agnosticism about evolution has successfully been constructed
as the moderate, open-minded position? If we are only asking about belief in evolution, then the answer is: probably not. Evolution is primarily

about what happened in the past, and although evolutionary theory is necessary to understand scientific phenomena today, such as antibiotic resistance, the widespread belief among evangelicals and fundamentalists in "microevolution," while problematic, is usually good enough to understand such processes. The rejection of evolution, in and of itself, probably does little damage to society or those who reject it. Sure, many people will go through life unacquainted with an elegant theory, and many potential biologists may be deterred from pursuing a career in science, but at the end of the day, it probably doesn't make a big difference.

But if we expand our scope beyond evolution, as any valid analysis must, then the answer must be that it matters immensely. Because the rejection of evolution in America is not in the last analysis simply a rejection of evolution; it is a centerpiece for the rejection of science itself. What the widespread rejection of evolution means to evangelical Christians and those who join them is that what scientists believe about the natural world doesn't really matter, especially when it's politically inconvenient—because after all, scientists believe in evolution, and "we all know that's not true." Anyone who doubts that this mentality exists and has political consequences need only look at evangelical thought on the other subjects discussed in this book. The evangelical campaign against embryonic stem cell research has extended beyond perfectly valid moral objections to destroying human embryos into a pseudoscientific campaign—led by David A. Prentice of the Family Research Council—claiming that there are no possible discoveries or treatments that would be closed off by forgoing embryonic stem cell research because adult stem cells can do it all and more. Evangelical antienvironmentalism—while mercifully abating in recent years, as many evangelical leaders have acknowledged, only a decade after it became the consensus view in the scientific community, that humans may be contributing to climate change—has been led by individuals such as E. Calvin Beisner of the Cornwall Alliance, who informs his evangelical followers that they needn't be concerned about the views that win out in the scientific marketplace of ideas because scientists are biased. Armed with a terminal degree in the history of Scotland, Beisner presumes to inform his evangelical followers on what the evidence *really* says about the environment ("The environment is improving, not deteriorating" in his analysis). And the evangelical campaign against homosexuality, led by James Dobson of Focus on the Family, has featured advocacy for measures that make it legal to deny secular jobs and housing to gay and lesbian people out of the supposition—rejected by all mainstream psychologists—that gays and lesbians have willfully chosen their orientation (and this is to say nothing of "conversion programs").

Does the widespread rejection of evolution matter?

You bet it does.

Epilogue:
Neo-Neo-Evangelicalism

THE ENTHUSIASM I EXPERIENCED upon embracing evangelical Christianity has dissipated considerably over the years. As college and graduate education gradually weakened my confidence in evangelicalism, I went through experiences that I know millions of other evangelical college students go through in America. Extra prayer requests were sent out on my behalf to family and friends because I had stepped across many of the symbolic boundaries that define the perimeter of the community (which was perceived as leaving the faith by many). Older evangelical leaders informed me that I was simply spiritually immature, or at the extreme end of a pendulum swing in my faith journey, and assured me that with time, learning, and maturity, I would eventually come to see things just like they did.

I used to believe that evangelical Christians really were bringing light to a dark culture, representing the author of truth, love, and harmony to a hurting, broken world. Now I believe evangelical Christianity has done more harm than good in the political sphere, that it has rallied behind beliefs that are untrue and supported policies that hurt others. My despair is deepened when I hear from other evangelicals like me, who went off to college, studied hard and tried to embrace a more nuanced version of

Christian faith, and found themselves returning home as outsiders, having failed too many of their culture's litmus tests for true belief.

But these rejected evangelicals also give me hope. In fact, they are in the same place as the evangelicals, several generations back, who broke off from Christian fundamentalism to form the evangelical Christianity of today. This episode in evangelical history provides disillusioned evangelicals both with hope that change can occur and with a possible strategy to bring about change.

During the 1940s and 1950s, a generation of disillusioned Christian fundamentalists came together to talk about their faith. They were dissatisfied with the fundamentalist community, with its isolation from the broader culture and intense suspicion toward different points of view, and envisioned a new kind of Christian community. Although they initially hoped to reform fundamentalist culture, they quickly discovered that this wouldn't work. All attempts to do so were met with intense resistance by the old guard, with cries of "heresy" and "liberalism," and with exclusion.

So this group of Christians decided to cut ties with fundamentalist culture and start anew. They didn't try to convince the older generation they were right. They didn't try to purge all the negative habits of the culture. They simply left and built a new home. This group started the evangelical Christianity of today, though it was known at the time as the neo-evangelical movement. It was a denominationally diverse but theologically conservative movement that coalesced around magazines like *Christianity Today*, leaders like Billy Graham, schools like Fuller Theological Seminary, and organizations like the National Association of Evangelicals. The idea was to present a new type of Christianity to the culture, a more reasonable and accommodating type.

The neo-evangelical movement has been remarkably successful in building churches and supporting mission work. It has also brought conservative Christians into contact with the broader culture, and awakened them to political activism. And it has also become politicized and reactionary and failed horribly on both ethical and scientific grounds. On the ethical front, neo-evangelicals have failed to confront social injustice in America, ignoring the civil rights movement, opposing the feminist movement, and dragging its feet for far too long in the face of environmental destruction. It has evinced prejudice and disgust toward gays and lesbians and shown no willingness to engage in dialogue with those who disagree on the matter. On the scientific front, the neo-evangelical movement has been in the forefront of crusades against evolution, supported untenable and destructive ideas about the nature of homosexuality, and demonstrated unwarranted skepticism about global warming and other environmental matters. It has exuded both ignorance and arrogance in the broader culture. In the process, it has made itself despised among the very people it seeks to convert to faith. It has also triggered a movement against itself—the new atheists—which argues, in effect, that if this is what Christianity looks like, we will all be better off when it goes extinct.

It remains to be seen whether today's evangelicalism can be reformed or whether the boundaries documented in this book, and the intellectual habits that support them, are too deeply ingrained, with too much momentum, to be purged from the culture. Hope comes from the evangelical about-face on environmentalism, its efforts to broaden the issue agenda beyond abortion and gay marriage, and signs that it is becoming less politicized and reactionary. Rick Warren has replaced James Dobson as the voice of evangelical culture.

Cause for concern comes from the fact that many of these new developments are justified by the same, naive belief in lens-free biblical interpretation that plagued the previous generation of evangelicals, by the fact that the culture still cares more about its celebrities than its scholars, it still refrains from serious dialogue with mainline Christians on topics like gay marriage, and still supports pseudoscientific ventures like intelligent design. And even Rick Warren says the difference between him and Dobson is more a matter of style than substance.

If neo-evangelicalism cannot be reformed, then disillusioned evangelicals should follow the model set by a previous generation of evangelicals. They should break ties with today's evangelical culture, take cries from the old guard of "liberal" and "heresy" with a large grain of salt, and start a new kind of evangelical Christianity. This would be an evangelical Christianity that embraces sound science, which requires ending the war against evolution. It would be an evangelical Christianity that recognizes the diverse expressions orthodox theology can take—from evangelicalism, to mainline Protestantism, to Catholicism and Greek Orthodox—but nevertheless carries on many distinctive features of the evangelical tradition. It would be an evangelical Christianity that realizes its reading of the Bible is always already governed by theology and politics, that cares more about the character of its adherents than whether or not they follow all the rules, that is more interested in the argument than the conclusion, and that puts more weight on the common beliefs that unite than the boundaries that divide.

It would be an evangelical Christianity worth believing in. It hasn't existed for a long time now. But it might exist again someday—hopefully soon.

ACKNOWLEDGMENTS

Numerous people and institutions made this book possible, either by contributing to my intellectual formation, helping me develop as a writer, or supporting me as I wrote. On the educational front, I want to thank the faculty of Calvin College for pushing its students—many of whom come from fundamentalist and conservative evangelical backgrounds—to think carefully and critically about their beliefs. My journey through Calvin has convinced me that a great many of the problems in evangelicalism today, and indeed, in American politics, would be alleviated if the professors at leading evangelical schools figured out how to better communicate their scholarship to lay evangelicals.

I want to single out Dale B. Martin, a professor of New Testament at Yale, for special thanks. His brilliant, delightful book *Sex and the Single Savior* had a huge impact on my thinking about biblical interpretation. Its impact is apparent in my discussions of each of the "big four" issues. Dale was an unflagging source of suggestions, constructive criticism, and encouragement throughout the process of writing and editing this book.

I want to thank Carol Pollard, associate director of Yale's Interdisciplinary Center for Bioethics, who suggested I write this book after reading one of my columns in the *Yale Daily News* and also helped guide me through the intimidating process of publishing a first book.

Many people read portions of the manuscript in its various stages and provided me with useful feedback: David H. Smith, Brian McLaren, Randall Balmer, Willis Jenkins, Keith DeRose, Stan Gundry, Jim Samara, Wes Mesko, Cherilyn Larsen, and the 2007 summer interns at Yale's Interdisciplinary Center for Bioethics. I am grateful to all of them. I should note that the views expressed in this book are not necessarily those of

Calvin College, Yale Divinity School, the Johns Hopkins School of Medicine, or anyone who read my manuscript.

On the writing front, I want to thank my agent Giles Anderson for believing in this project, helping me hone my writing style, and guiding me through the publishing process. I want to thank the entire team at Crown—including Trace Murphy, John Burke, Darya Porat, Laurie McGee, Rachelle Mandik, and the marketing department—for guiding this project to completion. I especially want to thank Gary Jansen, who served as my editor. This book is infinitely more readable as a result of his thoughtful advice.

On the supportive front, I want to thank my girlfriend Sara Madanikia—a fellow Hopkins med student—for putting up with my frequent preoccupation as I finished editing this book, critically reading many portions, and being a great source of encouragement through the tail end of this project. I want to thank my sisters, Loralee (who insisted she be identified as a peace-loving hippie somewhere in the manuscript) and Cherilyn, for their friendship and ideological kinship. Finally, I want to thank my mom and dad. Despite their hesitation about the ideas behind the book, they provided me with room and board while I finished it and were always willing to read my drafts and hear my arguments. For their love and generosity, and for putting up with my recalcitrance for many years, I'm dedicating this book to them.

NOTES

CHAPTER ONE: THE BIBLE, BIOLOGY, AND BOUNDARIES

Page 12—*When evangelical pastor Greg Boyd*   With the exception of the Greg Boyd situation, all these episodes are discussed further in the coming chapters. Greg Boyd's book was *The Myth of a Christian Nation: How the Quest for Political Power Is Destroying the Church* (Grand Rapids: Zondervan, 2007). See also Laurie Goodstein, "Disowning Conservative Politics, Evangelical Pastor Rattles Flock," in the *New York Times*, July 30, 2006.

Page 20—*Ross Douthat, a* New York Times *columnist, laments*   Ross Douthat, "Theocracy, Theocracy, Theocracy," in *First Things*, August/September 2006, 23–30.

Page 20—*As historian Mark Noll writes*   Mark Noll, *The Scandal of the Evangelical Mind* (Grand Rapids: Wm. B. Eerdmans, 1994). Quotes are from pages 3–4, 15–16.

Page 21—*As Notre Dame sociologist Christian Smith observes*   Christian Smith, *American Evangelicalism: Embattled and Thriving* (Chicago: University of Chicago Press, 1998), 126, 127.

Page 21—*After summarizing several polls, Georgetown political scientist Clyde Wilcox makes a similar observation*   Clyde Wilcox and Carin Larson, *Onward Christian Soldiers? The Religious Right in American Politics* (Boulder: Westview Press, 2006), 138.

Page 22—*Perhaps that's why, as* New York Times *columnist Nicholas Kristof has observed*   Nicholas Kristof, "Evangelicals a Liberal Can Love," *New York Times*, February 3, 2008.

CHAPTER TWO: PRO-LIFE PROSELYTIZING

Page 25—*"Make no mistake about it"*   William Lane Craig, *Hard Questions, Real Answers* (Wheaton: Crossway Books, 2003), 118, 126, 127. Craig's suggestion that the embryo should be considered an ensouled human person because it is human life with a unique set of chromosomes runs into the problem that hytidaform moles, tumors that form from some embryos, are also human life with a unique set of chromosomes. Are they also therefore human persons? These scientific aspects are discussed below.

155

Page 25—*Likewise, Rick Warren*   Beliefnet.com, "Rick Warren on His Saddle-
back Summit with McCain and Obama," http://www.beliefnet.com/News/
Politics/2008/08/Rick-Warren-On-His-Saddleback-Summit-With-Mccain-
And-Obama.aspx. See also Steven Waldman's interview of Warren, cited below.

Page 25—*A regular contributor for* Christianity Today   Stan Guthrie, "When Red Is
Blue: Why I Am Not a Red-Letter Christian," *Christianity Today* 51, no. 10 (October
2007).

Page 26—*The magazine, which is the biggest*   Ted Olsen, "Where Jim Wallis Stands,"
Christianity Today 52, no. 5 (May 2008).

Page 26—*A few pages later*   Stan Guthrie, "We're Not Finished: Abortion Is Not
Simply One Item on Our Social Agenda," *Christianity Today* 52, no. 5 (May 2008).

Page 27—*In this light, most of the popular pro-choice arguments fail*   I think Judith
Jarvis Thomson's famous article, "A Defense of Abortion," is an exception to this
statement. Thomson argues that abortion should be legal even if the fetus is a person from conception onward. I choose to ignore Thomson's article in this chapter,
however, in part because I want to focus more on religious aspects of abortion
than legal aspects and in part because the type of abstract philosophical reasoning
she engages in tends not to find purchase with evangelicals. Thomson's article, "A
Defense of Abortion," can be found in Joel Feinberg (ed.), *The Problem of Abortion*
(Belmont, CA: Wadsworth, 1973).

Page 27—*As ethicist Lew Smedes rightly notes*   Lewis B. Smedes, "CT Classic: Arguments in Favor of Abortion Are Strong . . . ," *Christianity Today* (July 1983),
accessed June 14, 2008, http://www.christianitytoday.com/ct/article_print.
html?id=7245.

Page 27—*"The reason I believe life"*   Steven Waldman, "Steven Waldman Interviews
Rick Warren," available from Beliefnet.com, accessed April 29, 2009, http://
www.beliefnet.com/News/2008/12/Rick-Warren-Transcript.aspx?p=1.
Warren compares abortion to the Holocaust in the same interview.

Page 27—*when then-presidential-candidate Barack Obama*   The exchange occurred
at "The Saddleback Civil Forum on Presidency" hosted by Warren, in which
he interviewed Obama and McCain in turn. The event was televised on CNN
on August 17, 2008. The responses of each candidate to Warren's question of
when fetal life begins featured prominently in Focus on the Family's e-newslet-
ter in October 2008, in which James Dobson declared that he would vote for
McCain.

Page 27—*Focus on the Family claims in its literature*   Accessed July 8, 2008, http://www.family.org/socialissues/A000001096.cfm.

Page 28—*Their sole cited support*   I should note that many past theologians did believe on the basis of other considerations that the incarnation occurred at conception and, although past theologians generally held that this was unique, others have used this fact to support the position that all moral life begins at conception (Cf. David Jones, "A Theologian's Brief on the Place of the Human Embryo within the Christian Tradition, and the Theological Principles for Evaluating Its Moral Status," in Brent Waters and Ronald Cole-Turner (eds.), *God and the Embryo: Religious Voices on Stem Cells and Cloning* (Washington, DC: George Washington University Press, 2003, 197).

Page 28—*The implicit suggestion that this verse provides us with information on when moral life begins*   Cf. George Marsden, "Why Creation Science?" *Understanding Fundamentalism and Evangelicalism* (Grand Rapids: Wm. B. Eerdmans, 1991), 153–181.

Page 28—*In its resolution against*   Southern Baptist Convention, "Resolution: On Human Embryonic and Stem Cell Research," in Waters and Cole-Turner (eds.), *God and the Embryo*, 179.

Page 30—*As one biblical scholar puts it*   Richard B. Hays, *Moral Vision of the New Testament: A Contemporary Introduction to New Testament Ethics* (New York: HarperSanFrancisco, 1996), 448. My interpretations here are informed by those of Hays as well as those of James C. Peterson in "Is a Human Embryo a Human Being?" in Waters and Cole-Turner (eds.), *God and the Embryo*, 78–87.

Page 30—*When we take the perspective*   Cynthia B. Cohen makes this point in "The Moral Status of Early Embryos and New Genetic Interventions," in David H. Smith and Cynthia B. Cohen (eds.), *A Christian Response to the New Genetics: Religious, Ethical, and Social Issues* (Lanham, MD: Rowman & Littlefield, 2003), 113.

Page 30—*due to genetic anomalies*   Errol R. Norwitz, Danny J. Shust, and Susan J. Fisher, "Implantation and the Survival of Early Pregnancy," *New England Journal of Medicine* 345, no. 19 (2001): 1400–1408; K. Hardy et al., "From Cell Death to Embryo Arrest: Mathematical Models of Human Preimplantation Embryo Development," *Proceedings of the National Academy of Sciences* 98, no. 4 (2001): 1655–1660; A. J. Wilcox, C. R. Weinberg, J. F. O'Connor, et al., "Incidence of Early Loss of Pregnancy," *New England Journal of Medicine* 319, no. 4 (1988): 189–194; Clifford Grobstein, "External Human Fertilization," *Scientific American* 240, no. 6 (1979): 57–67. I get these references from Ibid., 128–37. These studies will be discussed further below.

Page 30—*In light of this fact, many Christian theologians*   Joseph F. Donceel, "Immediate Animation and Delayed Hominization," *Theological Studies* 31 (1970): 76–105. See 100–177 for a discussion of the positions of Rahner and Anselm.

Page 30—*Willem A. VanGemeren*   Quoted in Michael Luo, "On Abortion, It's the Bible of Ambiguity," *New York Times*, November 13, 2005. Gilbert Meilaender, who served on George W. Bush's bioethics council and is a firm opponent of abortion from conception onward, also concedes this point in *Bioethics: A Primer for Christians* (Carlisle, UK: Paternoster, 1996), 29.

Page 30—*Richard B. Hays*   Hays, *Moral Vision*, 446.

Page 30—*Pope John Paul II*   Pope John Paul II, *Evangelium Vitae* (The Gospel of Life) (New York: Random House, 1995), 108. I initially came across this statement in Peterson, "Is a Human Embryo a Human Being?" in Waters and Cole-Turner (eds.), *God and the Embryo,* 80.

Page 31—*Orthodox Judaism is famous*   For one discussion of Jewish practices, see Rob Bell, *Velvet Elvis: Repainting the Christian Faith* (Grand Rapids: Zondervan, 2005), 126–127.

Page 32—*This position is justified*   Cynthia B. Cohen, "The Moral Status of Early Embryos and New Genetic Interventions," in Cohen and Smith (eds.), *A Christian Response to the New Genetics*, 107; Laurie Zoloth, "'Each One an Entire World': A Jewish Perspective on Family Planning," in Daniel C. Maguire (ed.), *Sacred Rights: The Case for Contraception and Abortion in World Religions* (New York: Oxford University Press, 2003), 38.

Page 32—*Thus, if the mother is having difficulty*   Speaking of her Jewish tradition, Zoloth notes, "If the mother's life, or physical or mental health, is at risk (including, for some, the situation in which having a severely disabled child, such as a child with Tay-Sachs, would threaten her mental health) the abortion is not only permitted, it is mandated." From "'Each One an Entire World'" in Maguire (ed.), *Sacred Rights,* 38–39.

Page 32—*As the Mishna*   Mishna, Oholot, 7, 6, cited in John Connery, *Abortion: The Development of the Roman Catholic Perspective* (Chicago: Loyola University Press, 1977), 15.

Page 32—*Because the fetus is not considered*   George Huntston Williams, "Religious Residues and Presuppositions in the American Debate on Abortion," *Theological Studies* 30 (1970): 10–75. On Jewish burial practices, see page 20.

Page 32—*These beliefs allow some Jews to recommend*   Cf. Zoloth, "'Each One an Entire World'" in Maguire (ed.), *Sacred Rights.*

Page 32—*Hence, at the beginning of former president George W. Bush's tenure* From "Cloning Research, Jewish Tradition and Public Policy: A Joint Statement by the Union of Orthodox Jewish Congregations of America and the Rabbinical Council of America," in Waters and Cole-Turner (eds.), *God and the Embryo,* 204–205.

Page 33—*The 2004 National Election Study poll* National Election Study 2004, referenced in Wilcox and Larson, *Onward Christian Soldiers?,* 58.

Page 34—*In 2002, Charles Colson* Cf. Charles Colson, *The Faith* (Grand Rapids: Zondervan, 2008), in which he presumes to set forth "what Christians believe." Colson argues, drawing on the Roman Catholic idea that life is sacred (a historically recent concept that is not found in the Bible) assumes without argument that having a high view of human life requires one to believe that moral life begins at conception and therefore that abortion is murder and should be criminalized. The same fallacious reasoning was employed by Francis Schaeffer and C. Everett Koop in *Whatever Happened to the Human Race?* (Wheaton: Crossway Books, 1979), discussed below.

Page 34—*teamed up with the fervently pro-life Richard Land of the Southern Baptist Convention to write a letter* See the letter at http://erlc.com/article/the-so-called-land-letter/. The letter was also signed by Bill Bright of Campus Crusade for Christ, James Kennedy of Coral Ridge Ministries, and Carl Herbster, president of the American Association of Christian Schools.

Page 34—*In* Christianity Today, *Colson wrote* Charles Colson, "The Back Page: Just War in Iraq," *Christianity Today* 46, no. 13 (December 9, 2002), accessed April 29, 2009, http://www.christianitytoday.com/ct/2002/december9/41.72.html.

Page 34—*Today's Religious Right leaders* Randall Balmer, *Thy Kingdom Come: How the Religious Right Distorts the Faith and Threatens America: An Evangelical's Lament* (New York: Basic Books, 2006), 17; Wilcox and Larson, *Onward Christian Soldiers?,* 61.

Page 35—*Early Christian views on when the soul* Donceel, "Immediate Animation."

Page 36—*The late Joseph Donceel, a philosophical theologian from Fordham University, explained it thus* Ibid., 83. I get the car/driver analogy from Donceel and also rely on him and Ronald Dworkin, *Life's Dominion: An Argument about Abortion, Euthanasia, and Individual Freedom* (New York: Vintage Books, 1993), for the explanation of the Plato/Aristotle difference in view on fetal life. I initially came across the quote from Donceel used here in Dworkin, *Life's Dominion,* 42.

Page 36—*Death is legally defined* For discussion, see Stuart J. Younger, Robert M. Arnold, and Renie Schapiro (eds.), *The Definition of Death: Contemporary Controversies* (Baltimore: Johns Hopkins University Press, 2002).

Page 36—*Anencephalic infants*　　　Cf. Arthur L. Caplan and Daniel H. Coelho, *The Ethics of Organ Transplants: The Current Debate* (New York: Prometheus Books, 1998), 80–115.

Page 36—*Occasionally, the embryo*　　　Cf. Ross S. Berkowitz and Donald P. Goldstein, "Molar Pregnancy," *New England Journal of Medicine* 360, no. 16 (2009): 1639–1645.

Page 37—*"If what is brought forth is unformed"*　　　Augustine, *Quaestionum in Hept*. I; II; n80. Quoted in G. R. Dunstan, "The Moral Status of the Human Embryo: A Tradition Recalled," *Journal of Medical Ethics,* no. 1 (1984): 38–44.

Page 37—*Augustine—who identified the image of God*　　　Augustine, *Literal Meaning of Genesis,* trans. and annot. John Hammond Taylor, 2 vols. (New York: Newman Press, 1982), 3.20.30. The full quote reads (with Augustine referring to the Genesis creation narratives): "From this, we are to understand that man was made to the image of God in that part of his nature wherein he surpasses the brute beasts. This is, of course, his reason or mind or intelligence, or whatever we wish to call it."

Page 37—*Jerome, for example, wrote*　　　Jerome, *Epistles*, 121.4, quoted in Cohen, "The Moral Status of Early Embryos," in Cohen and Smith (eds.), *A Christian Response,* 110.

Page 37—*Gregory of Nyssa declared*　　　Gregory of Nyssa, *Adversus Macedonianos*, ed. H. Walce and P. Schaff (Oxford and New York: Library of Nicene and Post-Nicene Fathers), series 2, vol. v, 1893: 320. I get this reference from G. R. Dunstan, "The Moral Status of the Human Embryo: A Tradition Recalled," *Journal of Medical Ethics* no. 1 (1984): 38–44.

Page 37—*Ambrosiaster, a disciple of Augustine*　　　Connery, *Abortion,* 58.

Page 38—*Anselm, a Catholic saint*　　　Quoted in Thomas A. Shannon and Allan B. Wolter, "Reflections on the Moral Status of the Pre-embryo." *Theological Studies*, 45(1990): 3–33.

Page 38—*Following Aristotle, Aquinas believed that the embryo goes through a number of early stages*　　　Ibid. Like the other theologians who followed Aristotle, Aquinas *did* believe the fetus was alive from the time of conception, with it initially having a life similar to a plant (implantation and growth in the uterus), then an animal (presence of rudimentary organs), then a human (sentient intellectual life). Each stage of life was animated by a soul appropriate for that level of biological development. As Aquinas states in his *Summa* (1, q. 76, a. 3, ad 3m): "The soul is in the embryo; the nutritive soul from the beginning; then the sensitive, lastly the intellectual soul." Also see Dworkin, *Life's Dominion,* 40–42. Dworkin includes a helpful discussion of the different interpretations surrounding Aquinas. Some have attempted to reconcile Aquinas's work with the idea that the soul is infused at or shortly after conception, most recently Jason T. Eberl, "Aquinas's Account of Human Embryogenesis and Recent Interpretations," *Journal of Medicine and Philosophy* 30 (2005): 379–394. Here, I accept the interpretation advanced in Donceel, "Immediate Animation"; Norman Ford, *When Did I Begin? Conception of the Human Individual in History, Philosophy and Science* (New York: Cambridge University Press, 1988); and Robert Pasnau, *Thomas Aquinas on Human Nature* (New York: Cambridge University Press, 2002). The recent attempts to reconcile Aquinas with the "life begins at conception" position must explain explicit statements made by Aquinas to the contrary, the history of interpretation of Aquinas as teaching the contrary, and the consensus of nearly all other past Christian thinkers, who drew on many of the same sources, on delayed hominization. My sense is also that these interpretations are not consistent with modern biological knowledge insofar as they posit that the embryo has inherent potential to develop into a sentient human being; this is not true because the potential of any embryonic cell is determined by the biological context in which it is located. Thus, in one context, stem cells will develop into heart muscle, in another, nerve cells, in another, skin cells, etc. And thus, the embryo does not have the potential to develop into sentient intellectual life apart from the womb because it continually receives nutrients and stimuli from its environment that regulate its gene expression. Also, it is quite likely that a skin cell nucleus, if transferred to an enucleated oocyte, could also drive the production of a cloned human in the uterus. If anything that has the potential to drive the production of a sentient human in some context should be treated as a human, then we very well may need to treat all our skin cell nuclei as humans. For these reasons, I also question claims that embryos produced outside the uterus via IVF should be treated with respect by virtue of their potential to become a human insofar as these claims also make the mistake of assuming that potential is something that can inhere in a cell, independently of its biological context.

Page 38—*This led him to conclude that* Cf. Donceel, "Immediate Animation." Donceel argues that "these conclusions have been reached, or could have been reached, on the basis of sound philosophical principles and of the common-sense biological knowledge which was available to Thomas and his contemporaries," 79.

Page 38—*As Aquinas states* *Summa Theologia,* Ia 76.5, also ST Ia 55.2; *Quaestiones disputatae de potentia dei* [QDP] III12; both cited in Eberl, "Aquinas's Account of Human Embryogenesis," 382. As the late Harvard theologian George Williams (who happened to oppose legalized abortion) noted, "Aquinas could not assert the full created humanity of the fetus until at least the rudiments of a human body and brain made plausible a rational animation thereof by the divine act of creation-infusion," in "Religious Residues," 30.

Page 38—*Where Aquinas went wrong*   Noonan notes, "[T]here was a period of fetal existence where Thomas' later writing did not specify the offense involved in fetal destruction yet where, according to his clear opposition to contraception, he believed a sin was being committed," John T. Noonan, Jr., "An Almost Absolute Value in History" in John T. Noonan, Jr. (ed.), *The Morality of Abortion: Legal and Historical Perspectives* (Cambridge: Harvard University Press, 1970), 23.

Page 39—*The Italian literary figure Dante*   A. J. Butler (ed. and tr.), *The Purgatory of Dante Alighieri* (London 1880), Canto 25, vv. 52–62, 67–75 (pp. 311–313), cited in Donceel, "Immediate Animation," 88–89.

Page 39—*The famous surgeon Thomas Vicary*   Dunstan, "Moral Status," 41.

Page 39—*The Roman Ritual*   Quotes from Donceel, "Immediate Animation," 89–90.

Page 39—*Alphonsus Liguori, a canonized doctor of the Church*   *Theologia Moralis* 6 (Bassani, 1779) tract. 2 no. 124, 107, cited in Donceel, "Immediate Animation," 91. Elswhere, Liguori writes: "On the other hand, some are mistaken who say that the fetus is ensouled from the first moment of its conception, since the fetus is certainly not animated before it is formed," quoted in ibid.

Page 39—*A Catholic theologian named H. M. Hering*   H. M. Hering, "De tempore animationis foetus humani," *Angelicum* 28 (1951): 18–19. I get this reference from Donceel, "Immediate Animation," 91.

Page 40—*Consistent with the long stream of theological thought*   Tim Stafford, "CT Classic: The Abortion Wars," *Christianity Today*, accessed June 14, 2008, http://www.christianitytoday.com/ct/article_print.html?id=7342;   "Brief of 281 American Historians as Amici Curiae Supporting Appellees," *The Public Historian*, 12, no. 3 (1990): 57–75. The irony, then, is that as Protestants started advocating "family values" they also, and for the same reasons, lost the traditional rationale for condemning early abortion.

Page 40—*Thus, James Wilson*   James Wilson, "Of the Natural Rights of Individuals," accessed September 9, 2010, http://teachingamericanhistory.org/library/index.asp?document=831.

Page 40—*Several nineteenth-century doctors*   Quoted in "Brief of 281 American Historians," 64.

Page 41—*Due to the high number*   Quoted in ibid., 70–72.

Page 41—*As James Mohr notes*   James C. Mohr, *Abortion in America: The Origins and Evolution of National Policy, 1800–1900* (New York: Oxford University Press, 1978), 90. Mohr notes, "Catholics did not practice abortion as a form of family limitation in the way that Protestants did" (91).

Page 41—*Indeed, the prevalence of abortion among Protestant women*   Cf. Ibid.; Kristin Luker, *Abortion and the Politics of Motherhood* (Berkeley: University of California Press, 1984); Joseph W. Dellapenna, *Dispelling the Myths of Abortion History* (Durham, NC: California Academic Press, 2005). Pro-life scholars tend to emphasize the belief that the embryo is human life as the main motivation while pro-choice scholars tend to emphasize the other factors cited. With the publication of Dellapenna's book on the subject, it appears the pro-life side has gained an upper hand in this particular debate, although I will argue below that belief in the "human life" of the embryo, by itself, does not entail any specific moral conclusions.

Page 41—*As Tim Stafford laments*   Stafford, "CT Classic: The Abortion Wars," *Christianity Today*, accessed June 14, 2008, http://www.christianitytoday.com/ct/article_print.html?id=7342.

Page 42—*During the 1960s, many were beginning to feel the laws*   Ibid.

Page 42—*In contrast to Roman Catholics (and some liberal Protestants)*   Liberal Protestants, content to develop their ethics at a further remove from strict literal readings of the Bible (and influenced as well by the strong antiabortion stance of their predecessors, Karl Barth and Dietrich Bonhoeffer), often adopted a more conservative stance on abortion than evangelicals. Among the mainline/liberal Protestants who opposed legalized abortion were John Noonan Jr. (University of California, Berkeley), George Huntston Williams (Harvard University), and Paul Ramsey (Princeton University). See John Noonan Jr. (ed.), *The Morality of Abortion: Legal and Historical Perspectives* (Cambridge: Harvard University Press, 1970). I should note that I do not discuss the work of Karl Barth and Dietrich Bonhoeffer in this history because, although I'm more inclined to side with their sophisticated theological reflection on abortion than the strict biblical literalism of evangelicals, I did not find any evidence that their views had a significant impact on the evangelical embrace of pro-life thought or politics in the late 1970s and early 1980s. Further, evangelical thought is much more similar to that of the Roman Catholic

Church, which does not officially allow an exception for rape, versus Karl Barth, who does (which does not make sense if one thinks all abortion is murder, as evangelicals do). Barth laments that "even Roman Catholic nuns raped when the Russians invaded Germany in 1945 were not allowed to free themselves from the consequences," calling the Roman Catholic position "horribly respectable" and "never sparing in its extreme demands on women" (and also criticized Catholic thought on the matter as "far too forbidding and sterile to promise any effective help"). And Bonhoeffer himself, although referring to the eugenically motivated abortions performed in Nazi Germany as "nothing but murder," nevertheless developed a more nuanced view elsewhere: "A great many different motives may lead to an action of this kind; indeed in cases where it is an act of despair, performed in circumstances of extreme human or economic destitution and misery, the guilt may often lie rather with the community than with the individual." Elizabeth Mensch and Alan Freeman, *The Politics of Virtue: Is Abortion Debatable?* (Durham: Duke University Press, 1993), 64, 65. I also note that many of the most influential theological descendants of Barth and Bonhoeffer today do not believe Christians should try to criminalize abortion (but rather, should refrain from practicing it themselves). See, for example, the work of Stanley Hauerwas and Richard Hays.

Page 42—*A leading professor of Old Testament from the famously conservative Dallas Theological Seminary*   Bruce Waltke, "The Old Testament and Birth Control," *Christianity Today,* 13, no. 3 (1968): 3–6.

Page 43—*Another professor from Dallas Theological Seminary—Norman Geisler*   Norman L. Geisler, *Ethics: Alternatives and Issues* (Grand Rapids: Zondervan, 1971), 219, 220. Quoted in Paul Fowler, *Abortion: Toward an Evangelical Consensus* (Portland: Multnomah Press, 1987), 76.

Page 43—*Articles in the evangelical* Christian Life *also drew on Exodus 21*   "Abortion— Is It Moral?" *Christian Life* 29, no. 5 (September 1967): 32–33, 50–53. I came across this quote in Jared Farley's doctoral dissertation, discussed below.

Page 43—*One professor of theology, writing in* Christianity Today, *urged*   Robert P. Meye, "The New Testament and Birth Control," *Christianity Today* 13, no. 3 (1968): 10–12.

Page 43—*In 1971, for example, the Southern Baptist Convention*   Quoted in Balmer, *Thy Kingdom Come*, 12. Also see Randall Balmer, *God in the White House: A History: How Faith Shaped the Presidency from John F. Kennedy to George W. Bush* (New York: HarperOne, 2008), 94.

Page 43—*Perhaps the most significant call for repeal*   Christian Medical Society, "A Protestant Affirmation on the Control of Human Reproduction," *Journal of the American Scientific Affiliation* 22 (June 1970): 46–47. The results of the symposium were also published in a book: Walter O. Spitzer and Carlyle L. Saylor (eds.), *Birth Control and the Christian* (Wheaton: Tyndale House, 1969). The trade-off between family life and fetal life is significant. Because evangelicals embraced a view of sex that elevates family life over celibacy and justifies contraception, they found themselves with little reason to uphold the premodern prohibition of early abortion—especially when doing so would conflict with "family values."

Page 44—*In 1975, a few evangelicals came together*   Quoted in Harding, *Book of Jerry Falwell,* 191.

Page 44—*As one founder of the CAC noted*   Quoted in Martin, *With God on Our Side,* 194.

Page 44—*Indeed, Jerry Falwell did not preach a sermon*   Harding, *Book of Jerry Falwell,* 303n5; Jared A. Farley, "The Politicization of the American Evangelical Press, 1960–1981: A Test of the Ideological Theory of Social Movement Mobilization" (PhD diss., Miami University, 2006, 36), accessed April 30, 2009, http://www.ohiolink.edu/etd/view.cgi?acc_num=miami1152903812.

Page 44—*A former president of the Southern Baptist Convention*   Quoted in Balmer, *Thy Kingdom Come,* 12–13.

Page 45—*the* Baptist Press *declared*   Quoted in Balmer, *Thy Kingdom Come,* 12–13.

Page 45—*With official teaching from the pope*   Dworkin, *Life's Dominion,* 44.

Page 45—*Thus, as late as 1980 the evangelical*   *Moody Monthly,* May 1980, 21. Quoted in Fowler, 75.

Page 45—*Randall Balmer, a professor of American religious history at Columbia University and editor at large for* Christianity Today, *has argued*   Balmer, *Thy Kingdom Come,* 13–17.

Page 46—*As Paul Weyrich*   Quoted in Martin, *With God on Our Side,* 173.

Page 46—*Weyrich's story*   Quoted in Balmer, *Thy Kingdom Come,* 12–17.

Page 47—*As Balmer notes*   Balmer, *Thy Kingdom Come,* 17.

Page 47—*Schaeffer, who held a master's degree*   Quoted in Garry Wills, *Head and Heart: American Christianities* (New York: Penguin Group, 2007), 485.

Page 47—*Later in his career, Schaeffer*   Norman Geisler, *The Creator in the Courtroom* (Fenton, MI: Mott Media, 1982), 205. Geisler notes, with some approval, "Francis Schaeffer in his recent book, *A Christian Manifesto* (Crossway, 1981), has called upon Christians to engage in civil disobedience and even use force to overcome the tyranny he sees implied in a negative decision in the Arkansas creation-evolution issue."

Page 47—*His main ministry began in Champéry, Switzerland*   Garry Wills, *Under God: Religion and American Politics* (New York: Simon & Schuster,. 1990), 322.

Page 48—*But Schaeffer would have none of it*   Quoted in Martin, *With God on Our Side*, 197.

Page 48—*In 1979, he cooperated with the surgeon C. Everett Koop*   Koop and Schaeffer, *Whatever Happened*; Harding, *Book of Jerry Falwell*, 189–194.

Page 48—Whatever Happened to the Human Race? *was somewhat of an affront*   A scene that crystallizes the ethos of the film involves Schaeffer reading from an academic paper advocating new views on abortion and then responding with incredulity into the camera. Koop has a similar scene. In other words, rather than responding to academic arguments with academic arguments, Schaeffer and Koop responded to them with demagoguery, going to the masses to stir up passions and resentment.

Page 49—*Schaeffer, who went by "Dr. Schaeffer"*   Harding points this out in *Book of Jerry Falwell*, 191–194. Schaeffer's community, L'Abri, declares "The first L'Abri community was founded in Switzerland in 1955 by Dr. Francis Schaeffer and his wife, Edith," http://www.labri.org/.

Page 49—*The book spent less than one paragraph*   Koop and Schaeffer, *Whatever Happened*.

Page 49—*Indeed, we are warned in the preface*   Koop and Schaeffer, *Whatever Happened*, xi.

Page 49—*The film featured booming horror-movie music*   C. Everett Koop and Francis Schaeffer, *Whatever Happened to the Human Race?* (DVD), initially produced by Gospel Communications, in 1979. This analysis is informed also by Harding, *Book of Jerry Falwell*, 192–93.

Page 50—*Schaeffer's views were widely disseminated*   Garry Wills, *Under God*, 324.

Page 51—*As political scientist Jared Farley notes*   Farley documents this entire process in his doctoral dissertation for Miami University, *The Politicization of the American Evangelical Press, 1960–1981*. The quote from Farley is from pages 127–128. The quotes from the Christian magazines are from pages 100, 95. See full reference above. Mark Noll also notes how one such periodical—*Christianity Today*—underwent a decrease in academic quality in order to stay afloat over the same period. As he writes in *Scandal of the Evangelical Mind* (15): "*Christianity Today*, which, for a decade or so after its founding in 1956, aspired to intellectual leadership, has been transformed into a journal of news and middle-brow religious commentary in order simply to stay in business." It appears, then, that the politicization of the American evangelical press was accompanied (in one major journal, at least) by a decrease in its academic quality.

Page 51—*One group, for example, distributed "Biblical Scorecards"*   Martin, *With God on Our Side*, 199.

Page 51—*Direct mailings often warned*   Quoted in Wilcox and Larson, *Onward Christian Soldiers?*, 11.

Page 52—*The Christian Coalition told followers*   Quoted in Ibid., 41.

Page 52—*In 1973, Catholics founded the National Right to Life Committee*   Dallas A. Blanchard, *The Anti-Abortion Movement and the Rise of the Religious Right: From Polite to Fiery Protest* (New York: Twayne Publishers, 1994), 39, 52, 62–63, 71, 78, 83–84.

Page 52—*In 1974, the Catholic Church*   Dworkin, *Life's Dominion*, 44.

Page 52—*While evangelicals were lying in*   Geoffrey Drutchas has argued in *Is Life Sacred?* (Cleveland: Pilgrim Press, 1990) that talk of the "sacredness of life" did not become part of mainstream Christian thought until the late nineteenth century. Richard B. Hays and Stanley Hauerwas have also critiqued talk of the "sacredness of life." Hays notes (*Moral Vision*, 454), "The 'sacredness of life' is a sacred cow that has no basis in the New Testament." Hauerwas affirms, "The Christian prohibition against taking life rests not on the assumption that human life has overriding value but on the conviction that it is not ours to take. . . . The Christian respect for life is first of all a statement, not about life, but about God" (quoted in Hays, *Moral Vision*, 455).

Page 53—*Several evangelical Right leaders*   Martin, *With God on Our Side*, 200.

Page 53—*Therefore, leaders of evangelical Right*   Ibid., 226–227.

Page 54—*Thus, when they emerged*   Cf. Cynthia Gorney, *Articles of Faith: A Front-line History of the Abortion Wars* (New York: Touchstone, 1998), 342. "Unlike their Catholic predecessors, who had worked so hard to convince others that the right-to-life position was rooted in science, logic, and broad moral principles rather than in religious training, the new evangelical recruits looked directly and openly to the Bible as they explained their reasoning to one another and the public around them."

Page 54—*One of the first instances of this phenomenon*   Jerry Falwell, *Listen America!* (Garden City: Doubleday, 1981), 165–180.

Page 54—*One of his direct mailers*   Harding, *The Book of Jerry Falwell*, 303–305, 304–16.

Page 55—*Other pro-life organizations*   Cf. Gorney, *Articles of Faith*.

Page 55—*According to one widely distributed*   Wilcox and Larson, *Onward Christian Soldiers?*, 142.

Page 55—*Hence, the outrage over a book titled* Brave New People   D. Gareth Jones, *Brave New People: Ethical Issues at the Commencement of Life* (Downers Grove, IL: Inter-Varsity Press, 1994).

Page 55—*Evangelical magazines and popular leaders*   Quoted in D. Gareth Jones, *Brave New People: Ethical Issues at the Commencement of Life,* rev. ed. (Grand Rapids: Wm. B. Eerdmans, 1985), xi–xii. See also "The View from a Censored Corner," in *Journal of the American Scientific Affiliation* 37 (September 1985): 169–177.

Page 56—*The popular response to the book*   Fowler, *Abortion*, 85.

Page 56—*In a preface, the author noted*   D. Gareth Jones, *Brave New People,* rev. ed., xvii–xviii.

Page 56—*A case in point is a book published*   Fowler, *Abortion,* 140, 135, 136–137, 140, 153. Equally tendentious books, also claiming that the Bible clearly says that life begins at conception, were published by John Jefferson Davis of Gordon-Conwell Theological Seminary in 1984 (*Abortion and the Christian,* Presbyterian and Reformed Publishing Company) and William Lane Craig of Talbot Theological Seminary in 1991 (*Hard Questions, Real Answers,* Crossway). Craig's chapter on abortion, which was first delivered as a sermon, instructs congregants to join the National Right to Life Committee and "vote for elected officials based on their pro-life stance." Arguments in favor of legalized abortion are "obviously unsound," "simply absurd," "scientific and medical poppycock," and "absolutely insane." Craig also claims that "abortion was never practiced among the Jews," apparently unaware that the Talmud commands abortion in some circumstances. "Some forty times the Scripture refers to conception as the start of new life in the womb," he writes. John Jefferson Davis argues that Christians should attempt to criminalize all abortions (including those for rape and incest) except when the mother's life is at risk and cites pro-life activist Harold O. J. Brown's remark about Psalm 139, Jeremiah 1, and Luke 1 that "God clearly says the unborn child is already a human being, made in the image of God and deserving the protection of the law." When it comes to a passage Jews have taken to support the life-begins-at-birth position, Davis abandons the insistence of a strict, literal construal that he brings to

Psalm 139 and Luke 1, insisting that this particular passage should not be "applied in a literalistic fashion" and that we should instead apply a strict literal reading only to the passages that might be used to support his position. "They are the ones to focus on," he adds.

Page 57—*A host of evangelical professors opposed*   Lewis B. Smedes, *Mere Morality* (Grand Rapids: Wm. B. Eerdmans, 1983), 143–144; Carl F. H. Henry, *The Christian Mindset in a Secular Society: Promoting Evangelical Renewal and National Righteousness* (Portland: Multnomah Press, 1984), 102–103; Robert N. Wennberg, *Life in the Balance: Exploring the Abortion Controversy* (Grand Rapids: Wm. B. Eerdmans, 1985), 165, following the famous "violin player" argument of Judith Jarvis Thomson, Wennberg declares, "The advocate of restrictive abortion legislation not only has to show that the fetus has a right to life but also has to show that the right to life includes the right to use another's body for life-sustaining purposes against that person's will" (155); Hessel Bouma III et al., *Christian Faith, Health, and Medical Practice* (Grand Rapids: Wm. B. Eerdmans, 1989), 232; Peterson in Waters and Cole-Turner (eds.), *God and the Embryo,* 79. Richard Hays, a theologically conservative scholar at Duke Divinity School, while opposing abortion in the Christian community, also opposed efforts to make it illegal in his influential book *The Moral Vision of the New Testament,* cf. 446, 457. I came across the statements from Smedes and Henry in Fowler, *Abortion,* 80–81.

Page 57—*After Calvin College professor*   Bouma informed me of this in personal conversation when I was a senior at Calvin, in the spring of 2006.

Page 57—*Wheaton College resisted attempts*   "Abortion to Be Resolved," *The Wheaton Record,* October 12, 1984, 2; *The Wheaton Record,* October 26, 1984; *The Wheaton Record,* January 25, 1985. One discussion of this episode is found in Fowler, *Abortion,* 82–84.

Page 58—*Even C. Everett Koop*   Martin, *With God on Our Side,* 241.

Page 59—*Thomas Aquinas, for example*   Cf. Donceel, "Immediate Animation," 78.

Page 59—*If having the capacity*   I get this point from Donceel, "Immediate Animation," 98. My discussion of the science here is also informed by Peterson, "Is a Human Embryo a Human Being?" in Waters and Coler-Turner (eds.), *God and the Embryo,* 82–85; Thomas A. Shannon and Allan B. Wolter, "Reflections on the Moral Status of the Pre-embryo," *Theological Studies* 51(4), 1990, 603–26; Carol A. Tauer, "The Tradition of Probabilism and the Moral Status of the Early Embryo," *Theological Studies* 45(1), 3–33; and Cynthia B. Cohen, "The Moral Status of Early Embryos and New Genetic Interventions," in Cohen and Smith (eds.), *A Christian Response to the New Genetics,* 105–30.

Page 60—*Due to hormone imbalances*   Norwitz, Shust, and Fisher, "Implantation and the Survival of Early Pregnancy"; Hardy et al., "From Cell Death to Embryo Arrest"; Wilcox, Weinberg, O'Connor, et al., "Incidence of Early Loss of Pregnancy"; and Grobstein, "External Human Fertilization." Also see Timothy F. Murphy, "The Moral Significance of Spontaneous Abortion," *Journal of Medical Ethics* 11 (1985): 79–83. I first came across this argument in Bouma et al., "Christian Faith," 37–40.

Page 61—*Granted, many of these embryos*   According to a 2002 World Health Organization study, HIV/AIDS kills 4.9% of people worldwide, malaria about 2.2%, and diabetes mellitus about 1.7%, www.who.int/whr/2004/annex/topic/en/annex_2_en.pdf. Accessed September 14, 2010.

Page 62—*These individuals have set fire to*   Cf. Blanchard, *The Anti-Abortion Movement.*

Page 62—*Other pro-life activists*   Cf. Blanchard, *Anti-Abortion Movement*; Thomas H. Murray, *Worth of a Child* (Berkeley: University of California Press, 1996): 147–152. Another killing occurred as I was revising this book, reported by Monica Davey and Joe Stumpe, "Doctor Who Provided Abortions Is Shot to Death," the *New York Times,* June 1, 2009.

Page 62—*A 1991 article in* Christianity Today, *titled*   Guy M. Condon, "You Say Choice, I Say Murder," *Christianity Today* 47 (January 2003), accessed April 29, 2009, http://www.christianitytoday.com/ct/2003/januaryweb-only/1-20-34.0.html.

Page 62—*Pro-life groups immediately condemned*   Murray, *Worth of a Child*, 150–151. My argument that pro-life activists are potentially being inconsistent in calling abortion mass murder and then condemning violence against it was inspired by a similar argument made by Murray on the same pages.

Page 63—*Because Hitler was presiding*   Interestingly, some of the more "extreme" (although I would say, "logically consistent") pro-life activists have referenced the case of Bonhoeffer to legitimate the use of extreme measures to end legalized abortion, including violence and murder. Cf. Garry Wills, *Under God.*

Chapter Three: Queer Quagmires

Page 66—*On August 19, 2009, a tornado*   Accounts of the incident come from http://minnesota.publicradio.org/display/web/2009/08/19/minneapolis

-tornado/ and http://www.desiringgod.org/Blog/1965_the_tornado_the_lutherans _and_homosexuality/.

Page 66—*For one local onlooker*   Desiring God Blog, John Piper, "The Tornado, the Lutherans, and Homosexuality," http://www.desiringgod.org/Blog/1965_the_ tornado_the_lutherans_and_homosexuality/.

Page 67—*One telling of the story*   Andrew Chignell, "Whither Wheaton?," http:// somareview.com/whitherwheaton.cfm.

Page 69—*In 1992, James Dobson worked*   Quoted in Balmer, *Thy Kingdom Come,* 25; William Stacy Johnson, *A Time to Embrace: Same-Gender Relationships in Religion, Law, and Politics* (Grand Rapids: Wm. B. Eerdmans, 2006).

Page 69—*His reasoning seemed simple enough*   Quoted in Jeff Lutes, *A False Focus on My Family,* 12, accessed August 13, 2009, http://www.soulforce.org/article/ false-focus-family.

Page 69—*Dobson's next major project*   Wilcox and Larson, *Onward Christian Soldiers?,* 71, 148.

Page 69—*"Focus on the Family is promoting the truth"*   Quoted in ibid., 10.

Page 69—*Previously, scientific arguments*   One survey of the scientific debate can be found in Stanton Jones and Mark Yarhouse, *Homosexuality: The Use of Scientific Research in the Church's Moral Debate* (Downers Grove, IL: InterVarsity Press Academic), 2000.

Page 70—*George W. Bush's reelection*   Daniel Smith, Matthew DeSantis, and Jason Kassel, "Same-Sex Marriage Ballot Measures and the 2004 Presidential Election," *State and Local Government Review* 38, no. 2 (2006): 78–91.

Page 70—*The measure defined*   See Lisa Leff, "Prop 8 Backer Questioned About Child Sex Comment," http://www.huffingtonpost.com/2010/01/13/historian -back-on-stand-i_n_421827.html.

Page 71—*D. A. Carson, a professor of New Testament*   D. A. Carson, *Becoming Conversant with the Emergent Church: Understanding a Movement and Its Implications* (Grand Rapids: Zondervan, 2005), 170–172.

Page 71—*In a book with a title that could summarize*   Daniel Helminiak, *What the Bible Really Says About Homosexuality* (San Francisco: Alamo Square Distributors, 2000).

Page 72—*Both parties to the debate about homosexuality*   Probably the most sophisticated biblical scholarship on the conservative side is from Richard B. Hays at Duke Divinity School: "Relations Natural and Unnatural: A Response to John Boswell's

Exegesis of Romans 1," *Journal of Religious Ethics* 14 (1986): 184–215; Hays, *The Moral Vision of the New Testament*, 379–406. Robert Gagnon's work is more comprehensive and up-to-date, though also more tendentious and reactionary: *The Bible and Homosexual Practices: Texts and Hermeneutics* (Nashville: Abingdon Press, 2001). Probably the best work on the liberal side comes from Dale B. Martin, *Sex and the Single Savior: Gender and Sexuality in Biblical Interpretation* (Louisville: Westminster John Knox, 2006); Diana M. Swancutt, "Sexy Stoics and the Rereading of Romans 1:18–2:16," in Amy-Jill Levine (ed.), *A Feminist Companion to Paul* (Cleveland: Pilgrim Press, 2004), 42–73; Swancutt, "'The Disease of Effemination': The Charge of Effeminacy and the Verdict of God (Rom. 1:18–2:16)," in Stephen D. Moore and Janice Capel Anderson (eds.), *New Testament Masculinities* (Boston: Brill Academic Publishers, 2004), 193–234; Swancutt, "Sexing the Pauline Body of Christ: Scriptural Sex in the Context of the American Christian Culture War," in Virginia Burrus and Catherine Keller (eds.), *Toward a Theology of Eros: Transforming Passion at the Limits of the Disciplines* (New York: Fordham University Press, 2006), 65–98; and Bernadette Brooten, *Love Between Women: Early Christian Responses to Female Homoeroticism* (Chicago: University of Chicago Press, 1998).

Page 72—*When liberal and conservative Christians expect*   Cf. Peter Harrison, *The Bible, Protestantism and the Rise of Natural Science* (Cambridge, UK: Cambridge University Press, 1998), 64–160; Noll, *Scandal of the Evangelical Mind,* 90. Chapter 4, "The Evangelical Enlightenment," in Noll's book is one of the most helpful sources for understanding this subject. See pages 83–108. See also Nancy Pearcey, *Total Truth: Liberating Christianity from Its Cultural Captivity* (Wheaton: Crossway Books, 2004), 295–323. This section and the next are informed by the following works: Mark A. Noll, *Between Faith and Criticism: Evangelicals, Scholarship, and the Bible in America* (Grand Rapids: Baker Book House, 1986); Mark A. Noll, "Common Sense Traditions and American Evangelical Thought" in *American Quarterly* 37(2): 216–238, 1985; George M. Marsden, *Fundamentalism and American Culture: The Shaping of Twentieth-Century Evangelicalism 1870–1925* (New York: Oxford University Press, 1980); George M. Marsden, *Understanding Fundamentalism and Evangelicalism* (Grand Rapids: Wm. B. Eerdmans, 1991); Nathan O. Hatch and Mark A. Noll (eds.), *The Bible in America: Essays in Cultural History* (New York: Oxford University Press, 1982); David N. Livingstone, D. G. Hart, and Mark A. Noll, *Evangelicals and Science in Historical Perspective* (New York: Oxford University Press, 1999); David N. Livingstone, *Darwin's Forgotten Defenders: The Encounter Between Evangelical Theol-*

ogy and Evolutionary Thought (Grand Rapids: Wm. B. Eerdmans, 1987); Ronald L. Numbers, *The Creationists: From Scientific Creationism to Intelligent Design,* expanded edition (Cambridge: Harvard University Press, 2006); Randall Balmer, *Mine Eyes Have Seen the Glory: A Journey into the Evangelical Subculture in America,* 4th ed. (New York: Oxford University Press, 2006); Nancey Murphy, *Beyond Liberalism and Fundamentalism: How Modern and Postmodern Philosophy Set the Theological Agenda* (Harrisburg: Trinity Press International, 1996); Del Ratzsch, *Science and Its Limits: The Natural Sciences in Christian Perspective* (Downers Grove, IL.: InterVarsity Press, 2000).

Page 73—*"I like a Biblical theology"*   "The Coming of the Lord: The Doctrinal Center of the Bible," *Addresses on the Second Coming of the Lord: Delivered at the Prophetic Conference, Allegheny, Pa., December 3–6, 1985* (Pittsburgh, 1985), 82. Quoted in George M. Marsden, *Fundamentalism and American Culture.*

Page 73—*This system of thought*   Herbert Hovenkamp, *Science and Religion in America, 1800–1860* (Philadelphia: University of Philadelphia Press, 1978), 5, 10. I get this reference and that below from Pearcey, *Total Truth,* 297. Incidentally, Pearcey has a fairly good overview of the material I am covering here in the same book, on 292–323. Despite that, she nevertheless applies a postfoundationalist approach to science and a foundationalist approach to the Bible, as I note below.

Page 74—*But this response failed*   George Marsden insightfully puts the problem this way in Marsden, *Fundamentalism and American Culture,* 220: "[I]f truth is so objective . . . how does one account for the wide prevalence of error? This was the great obstacle to the whole Common Sense philosophy and the rock against which in the nineteenth century it repeatedly foundered, until all but its most stubborn exponents were dislodged. How is it that there are so many rational and upright people of good will who refuse to see truth which consists of objective facts that are plain as day?"

Page 74—*Following the Dutch theologian and politician*   Cf. Abraham Kuyper, *Principles of Sacred Theology*, trans J. Hendrick De Vries (Grand Rapids: Baker Book House, 1980). The contrast between Baconian and Kuyperian understandings of interpretation and their relation to the evangelical community is explained well in Marsden, "The Evangelical Love Affair with Enlightenment Science," in *Understanding Fundamentalism and Evangelicalism*, 122–152. See also Marsden, *Fundamentalism and American Culture*, 115; Pearcey, *Total Truth,* 313; Noll, *Between Faith and Criticism: Evangelicals, Scholarship, and the Bible in America* (Grand Rapids: Baker Book House, 1986), 32–162.

Page 76—*Rather than arguing that creationism*   Ronald Numbers notes: "The 1970's witnessed a major shift in creationist tactics. Instead of trying to outlaw evolution, as they had done in the 1920's, antievolutionists now fought to give creation equal time. And instead of appealing to the authority of the Bible, as Morris and Whitcomb had done as recently as 1961, they consciously downplayed the Genesis story in favor of what they called 'scientific creationism.' . . . In defending creation as a scientific alternative to evolution, creationists relied less on Francis Bacon and his conception of science and more on two new philosopher-heroes, Karl Popper and Thomas Kuhn. . . . This tactic proved extremely effective. Two state legislatures and various school boards adopted the two-model approach, and an informal poll of school board members in 1980 showed that only 25 percent favored teaching nothing but evolution" (543), in Ronald L. Numbers, "Creationism in 20th-Century America," *Science* 218, no. 5 (1982): 538–544. See also *The Creationists: From Scientific Creationism to Intelligent Design*, expanded ed. (Cambridge: Harvard University Press, 2006), 274–275, 369.

Page 76—*Thus, in a 1974 article in the young earth creationist journal*   Leonard R. Brand, "A Philosophic Rationale for a Creation-Flood Model," *Origins* 1, no. 2 (1974): 73–83. See also Ariel A. Roth, "The Pervasiveness of the Paradigm," *Origins* 2, no. 2 (1975): 55–57; John W. Klotz, *Studies in Creation: A General Introduction to the Creation / Evolution Debate* (St. Louis: Concordia Publishing House, 1985), 20–22. I found these sources via Numbers, *The Creationists*, 514.

Page 76—*Phillip Johnson, widely considered*   Johnson, "Foreword," in Pearcey, *Total Truth,* 12.

Page 76—*Evolution, he argues, is*   Phillip E. Johnson, "Evolution as Dogma," in Robert T. Pennock (ed.), *Intelligent Design Creationism and Its Critics: Philosophical, Theological, and Scientific Perspectives* (Cambridge, MA: MIT Press, 2001), 59–76, quote from 60.

Page 77—*Evangelical philosopher Nicholas Wolterstorff*   Nicholas Wolterstorff, *Reason Within the Bounds of Religion* (Grand Rapids: Wm. B. Eerdmans, 1976), 73.

Page 77—*Likewise, evangelical philosopher Alvin Plantinga*   Alvin Plantinga, "When Faith and Reason Clash: Evolution and the Bible" and "Methodological Naturalism?" both in Pennock (ed.), *Intelligent Design Creationism and Its Critics,* 113–146; 339–362. The quotes are from 123, 343, and 123, respectively. Plantinga cites Kuyper and others as inspiration for his position.

Page 77—*In an article titled*   Alvin Plantinga, "Two (or More) Kinds of Scripture Scholarship," in *Warranted Christian Belief*, 374–421.

Page 77—*Evangelical Bible scholar Peter Craigie*   Peter C. Craigie, "The Role and Relevance of Biblical Research," *Journal for the Study of the Old Testament* 18 (1980): 29. Quoted in Noll, *Between Faith and Criticism*, 183.

Page 78—*As historian Mark Noll has pointed out*   Noll, *Scandal of the Evangelical Mind,* 197. To be sure, there are some evangelicals who still retain ideas of objectivity and universality in science and historical work, but as far as I can tell, they are a distinct minority, are mainly confined to Bible schools and fundamentalist seminaries, and have little influence on the mainstream evangelical community. James K. A. Smith makes a similar observation in "Who's Afraid of Postmodernism? A Response to the 'Biola School'" in Myron Penner (ed.), *Christianity and the Postmodern Turn*, 215–228.

Page 78—*What this means in practice is that*   Leonard R. Brand, "A Philosophic Rationale for a Creation Flood Model," *Origins* 1 (1974): 73–83; see also Ariel A. Roth, "The Pervasiveness of the Paradigm," *Origins* 2 (1975): 55–57.

Page 78—*As creationist Henry Morris writes*   Henry M. Morris, *Biblical Cosmology and Modern Science* (Grand Rapids: Baker Book House, 1970), 32–33.

Page 78—*It means that when evangelical Right activists*   Pearcey, *Total Truth*, 41.

Page 79—*When they want their construal of biblical morality*   Ibid., 24.

Page 79—*It means that when the provost of Wheaton College*   Mark A. Yarhouse and Stanton L. Jones, "A Critique of Materialist Assumptions in Interpretations of Research on Homosexuality," in *Christian Scholar's Review* 26, no. 4 (1997): 478–495. The article following that by Jones and Yarhouse in the same journal has a similar theme, with the title: "Taking Our Assumptions Out of the Closet." Seeking to examine "the implications of five major assumptions for interpreting and applying scientific research on homosexuality," the author concludes, "thinking differently about these assumptions affects interpretation of the results." "Researchers and interpreters of research," the author notes, in a summary statement, "must learn to reflect critically on the social, cultural and political contexts which shape" the interpretation of "this supposedly 'objective' scientific research." Heather Looy, "Taking Our Assumptions Out of the Closet: Psychobiological Research on Homosexuality and Its Implications for Christian Dialogue," *Christian Scholar's Review* 26, no. 4 (1997): 496–513.

Page 79—*When he wants to fault the biblical interpretations*   Jones and Yarhouse, *Homosexuality*, 178.

Page 80—*As Merold Westphal*   Merold Westphal, *Whose Community? Which Interpretation? Philosophical Hermeneutics for the Church* (Grand Rapids: Baker Academic, 2009), 14.

Page 82—*Liberal scholars point out*   One example of this approach can be found in the work of Martin, Swancutt, and Brooten, cited above. See, for example, Martin, *Sex and the Single Savior,* 59–60.

Page 82—*Paul's only other*   Martin, Ibid.

Page 82—*The debate over gay marriage ultimately hinges*   These (usually unspoken) rules for biblical interpretation are helpfully elucidated in Charles H. Cosgrove, *Appealing to Scripture in Moral Debate: Five Hermeneutical Rules* (Grand Rapids: Wm. B. Eerdmans, 2002).

Page 83—*What cultural factors and lenses lead evangelicals to interpret the Bible as condemning gay unions?*   A similar question could be asked about why liberal Christians interpret the Bible as allowing gay marriage. This question should be asked, and answered, to avoid giving the impression that conservatives are biased by cultural factors in this debate whereas liberals are not. Unfortunately, answering such a question is outside of the scope of this book, which is focused on assessing and critiquing evangelicalism.

Page 84—*As late as 2003, Focus on the Family*   Joseph Nicolosi, Focus on the Family's "Love Won Out" conference, Oklahoma City, 2003. Cited in Jeff Lutes, *A False Focus on My Family*, 4, accessed August 13, 2009, http://www.soulforce.org/article/false-focus-family.

Page 84—*Today most evangelical leaders*   CNN, November 22, 2006, 21:00 ET, *Larry King Live.* The statement is a response to Larry King's question "Do you still believe that being gay is a choice?"

Page 84—*The president of the Southern Baptist Convention*   Quoted in Michael Lindenberger, "An Evangelical's Concession on Gays," *TIME*, Mar. 16, 2007, accessed September 23, 2008, http://www.time.com/time/printout/0,8816,1599987,00.html.

Page 84—*Most scientists, on the right and the left*   One survey of the evidence, from an evangelical who opposes homosexuality, can be found in Jones and Yarhouse, *Homosexuality*.

Page 84—*"We want people to know that individuals don't have to be gay"*   Cited in Lutes, *False Focus*, 10.

Page 85—*Even many far-right evangelicals are*   Tim Stafford, "An Older, Wiser, Ex-Gay Movement: The 30-Year-Old Ministry Now Offers Realistic Hope for Homosexuals," *Christianity Today*, September 13, 2007. The article summarizes changes in evangelical thinking over the past thirty years.

Page 85—*A 2000 poll of small Republican donors*   Wilcox and Larson, *Onward Christian Soldiers?*, 63, 136–137, 150–151, 161.

Page 85—*This is the culture in which evangelical scholars*   Quoted in Andrew Chignell's "Wither Wheaton?," http://www.somareview.com/whitherwheaton .cfm.

Page 86—*Profamily organizations are founded on the belief*   Cf. The Ramsey Colloquium, "The Homosexual Movement: A Response by the Ramsey Colloquium," accessed September 9, 2010, at www.orthodoxytoday.org/articles/Ramsey Homosexuality.php.

Page 86—*Evangelical leaders regularly insist*   Cf. Jones and Yarhouse, *Homosexuality*, 46.

Page 86—*Yet the same leaders nevertheless state*   Quoted in Jeff Lutes, *A False Focus on My Family*, Soulforce, 6. For the full quote pertaining to the earth: "Homosexuals are not monogamous. They want to destroy the institution of marriage. It will destroy marriage. It will destroy the Earth." In *The Daily Oklahoman*, Oct. 23, 2004. Martin develops this point in *Sex and the Single Savior*, 62–63.

Page 86—*But as Mark Noll notes*   Noll, *Between Faith and Criticism*, 151, 153.

Page 87—*A popular refrain in the gay debate is that Christians*   Some of these points are made by Robert C. Dykstra of Princeton Theological Seminary in *Frequently Asked Questions About Sexuality, the Bible, & the Church* (San Francisco: Covenant Network of Presbyterians, 2006), 99.

Page 88—*In response to the creationists of his day, Augustine*   Augustine, *Literal Meaning of Genesis*, 1:42–43. My discussion here is informed by Noll, *Scandal of the Evangelical Mind,* 202–203.

Page 89—*Augustine states that passages*   Augustine, *On Christian Doctrine,* 1.35.40, 3.55. Quoted in Martin, *Sex and the Single Savior,* 12, 168.

Page 89—*Such interpretations are true*   St. Augustine, *Christian Doctrine*, 1.36.40. My analysis in this paragraph is informed both by Dale Martin's discussion in chapters 1 and 11 of *Sex and the Single Savior* and by James K. A. Smith's discussion in *The Fall of Interpretation*.

CHAPTER FOUR: ENVIRONMENTAL EXPERIENCES

Page 91—*In a document by the group*   The document can be accessed at http://www. cornwallalliance.org/articles/read/the-cornwall-declaration-on-environmental-stewardship/. My analysis here is informed by Balmer, *Thy Kingdom Come*, 153–155.

Page 91—*Richard Cizik*   Cf. Adelle M. Banks, "Dobson, Others Seek Ouster of NAE Vice President," accessed May 25, 2009, http://www.christianitytoday. com/ct/2007/marchweb-only/109–53.0.html; Gregory Tomlin, "Letter Asks NAE to Rethink 'Green' Activism," *Baptist Press*, March 9, 2007, accessed May 25, 2009, http://www.bpnews.net/bpnes.asp?ID=25144.

Page 92—*In December of 2008, after twenty-eight years*   Dan Gilgoff, "Moderate Evangelical Richard Cizik's Resignation May Not Stop Broadening of the Evangelical Agenda," *U.S. News & World Report*, December 12, 2008. Accessed online at politics.usnews.com, November 11, 2010.

Page 93—*The consequences of this interpretation*   Quoted in Balmer, *Thy Kingdom Come*, 148. The assessment of the environmental argument against Christianity is informed by Steven Bouma-Predger, *For the Beauty of the Earth* (Grand Rapids: Baker Academic, 2001) 67–86.

Page 93—*"Biblical Christians"*   E. Calvin Beisner, *Where Garden Meets Wilderness: Evangelical Entry into the Environmental Debate* (Grand Rapids: Acton Institute and Wm. B. Eerdmans, 1997), 107.

Page 94—*Ross Douthat*   Ross Douthat, "The Right and the Climate," *New York Times*, July 25, 2010.

Page 95—*This change is apparent*   Available at http://www.baptistcreationcare .org/. These developments are discussed from a conservative/fundamentalist perspective in Brent McCracken, "The Greening of Evangelicals," *Biola Magazine*, Fall of 2008. Accessed September 9, 2010, http://www.biola.edu/news/biola mag/articles/08fall/greening.cfm.

Page 95—*As* Christianity Today *puts it*   "It's Not Easy Being Green," *Christianity Today*, quoted in Robert Booth Fowler, *The Greening of Protestant Thought* (Chapel Hill: University of North Carolina Press, 1995), 40.

Page 95—*What about the earth being destroyed*   R. J. Berry, in R. J. Berry (ed.), *The Care of Creation: Focusing Concern and Action* (Downers Grove, IL: InterVarsity Press, 2000), 180.

Page 95—*As Calvin DeWitt writes*   Calvin DeWitt, in ibid., 71.

Page 96—*Ron Sider*   Ron Sider, in ibid., 45–46.

Page 96—*Thomas Derr, currently a professor*   Fowler, *Greening,* 38. I should note here that this is not a quote from Derr but a summary of concerns Derr expresses in one of his books. This criticism has also been raised against the "green Bible" published by HarperOne in 2008.

Page 96—*Aside from the Genesis 1:28 command*   This analysis is informed by the work of Fowler (37), Beisner (54–57), and Singer (56), cited in full elsewhere in this chapter's endnotes.

Page 96—*in the original language*   Harrison, "Subduing," 88.

Page 97—*To be sure, there are some exceptions*   H. Paul Santmire, in *The Travail of Nature: The Ambiguous Promise of Christian Theology* (Minneapolis: Fortress Press, 1985), gives an assessment of both positive and negative attitudes toward the environment in the Christian tradition. In my opinion, he plays up positive aspects and de-emphasizes negative ones to give a portrait of the tradition more "ambiguous" than it actually is. But it is nevertheless a helpful survey of the tradition and a needed corrective to the tendency of many histories to portray the tradition as monolithically negative.

Page 97—*Augustine wrote that man*   Augustine, *City of God*, XXII.24, 851; *The Catholic and Manichean Ways of Life*, XVII (*FC* 56, 102, 105). Quoted in Harrison, *The Bible, Protestantism and the Rise of Natural Science*, 177.

Page 98—*Augustine pointed to the Gospels*   Augustine, *The Catholic and Manichean Ways of Life*, 102. I discovered many of these discussions in Peter Singer in "Not for Humans Only: The Place of Nonhumans in Environmental Issues," in Andrew Light and Holmes Rolston III (eds.), *Environmental Ethics: An Anthology* (Malden, MA: Blackwell Publishing, 2003), 55–64.

Page 98—*Aquinas reaffirmed Augustine's views*   Thomas Aquinas, *Compendium of Theology* 148; *Summa Theologica,* 1.96.1, quoted in Santmire, *The Travail of Nature*, 91.

Page 98—*Animal abuse is not inherently wrong*   *Summa Contra Gentiles*, III, II, 112. I get this reference from Peter Singer, "Not for Humans Only," in Light and Rolston (eds.), *Environmental Ethics*, 56.

Page 98—*His contemporary, Hildegard of Bingen*   Hildegard, *Liber divinorum operum* 1.iv.100, quoted in Harrison, *Protestantism*, 54–72.

Page 98—*The medieval theologian Bonaventure*   Bonaventure, *Breviloquium* 2.4, quoted in Harrison, *Protestantism*, 178.

Page 98—*Even Francis of Assisi*   St. Francis of Assisi, *His Life and Writings as Recorded by His Contemporaries*, tr. L. Sherely-Price (London, 1959), quoted in Singer, "Not for Humans Only," in Light and Rolston (eds.), *Environmental Ethics*, 56.

Page 98—*Continuing in this tradition, John Calvin*   Calvin, *Commentaries on the First Book*, 64, quoted in Santmire, *The Travail of Nature*, 125.

Page 98—*Martin Luther agreed*   Luther, *Lectures on Genesis (Chapters 1–5)*, Vol. 1 of *Luther's Works*, ed. Jaroslav Pelikan (St. Louis: Concordia Publishing House, 1955), 47, quoted in Santmire, *Travail of Nature*, 124 and in Harrison, *The Bible, Protestantism and the Rise of Natural Science* (Cambridge: Cambridge University Press, 1998), 178.

Page 98—*One study found that Christians*   Reported in Fowler, *The Greening of Protestant Thought*, 25.

Page 98—*An independent study came*   Quoted in ibid., 25.

Page 98—*According to a 2007 Barna poll*   Quoted in Alexis Madrigal, "Bishops Tell Christians to Give Up Some Carbon for Lent," in *Wired,* February 7, 2008, accessed July 18, 2009, http://www.wired.com/wiredscience/2008/02/bishops-tell-ch/.

Page 99—*Obviously, we wouldn't expect*   R. J. Berry in Berry (ed.), *The Care of Creation,* 177.

Page 99—*But the word "stewardship" is not found in the Bible in discussions of nature*   Bauckham, "Stewardship and Relationship" in *Creation,* 99.

Page 100—*During four different eras of history*   Harrison, *The Bible, Protestantism and the Rise of Natural Science*; Peter Harrison, "Having Dominion: Genesis and the Mastery of Nature," in *Environmental Stewardship: Critical Perspectives—Past and Present* (London: T&T Clark, 2006), 17–31; Peter Harrison, "Subduing the Earth: Genesis 1, Early Modern Science, and the Exploitation of Nature," *The Journal of Religion* 79, no. 1 (1999): 86–109; Peter Harrison, "'Fill the Earth and Subdue It': Biblical Warrants for Colonization in Seventeenth Century England," *Journal of Religious History* 29 (2005): 3–24. Most of the quotes from past theologians in the texts were discovered through Harrison's scholarship, unless another contemporary author is indicated. Other helpful discussions of the subject (covering either ancient or modern interpretations) include Jeremy Cohen, *"Be Fertile and Increase, Fill the Earth and Subdue It": The Ancient and Medieval Career of a Biblical Text* (Ithaca: Cornell University Press, 1989); John Passmore, *Man's Responsibility for Nature: Ecological Problems and Western Traditions* (London: Duckworth, 1974); Peter Harrison, *The Fall of Man and the Foundations of Science* (Cambridge: Cambridge University Press, 2007); Santmire, *The Travail of Nature*; H. Paul Santmire, *Nature*

Reborn: The Ecological and Cosmic Promise of Christian Theology (Minneapolis, Fortress Press, 2000); Richard Bauckham, "Modern Domination of Nature—Historical Origins and Biblical Critique," in Berry (ed.), *Environmental Stewardship*, 32–50; Richard Bauckham, "Stewardship and Relationship," in Berry (ed.), *The Care of Creation*, 99–106; Clare Palmer, "Stewardship: A Case Study in Environmental Ethics," in Berry (ed.), *Environmental Stewardship*, 63–76; Fowler, *The Greening of Protestant Thought*; and Beisner, *Where Garden Meets Wilderness*, especially 1–8.

Page 100—*The theologian Origen*   Quoted in Harrison, "Genesis and the Mastery of Nature," in Berry (ed.), *Environmental Stewardship*, 19.

Page 100—*The fall of mankind into sin was thought*   Augustine, *Confessions*, 13.21. Quoted in Ibid.

Page 100—*And likewise, John Chrysostom*   John Chrysostom, *Homilies on Genesis*, VIII. 14. Quoted in Ibid.

Page 100—*Harrison summarizes*   Harrison, "Subduing the Earth," 91.

Page 101—*The idea of a "book of nature," Harrison writes*   Harrison, *The Bible, Protestantism and the Rise of Natural Science*, 45.

Page 101—*The Genesis 1:28 command to "subdue the Earth" and "have dominion" over the beasts*   Bonaventure, Hexameron, 13. Quoted in Harrison, "Genesis and the Mastery of Nature," in Berry (ed.), *Environmental Stewardship*, 21.

Page 102—*As Harrison notes,*   Harrison, "Subduing," 93.

Page 102—*Francis Bacon thus wrote*   Bacon, *The Interpretation of Nature*, in *Works*, III 224. Quoted in Harrison, *The Bible*, 104.

Page 102—*Whereas scientists had once studied nature*   Harrison, *The Bible*, 64–160.

Page 103—*As Bacon declared*   Bacon, *Novum Organum*, 2.52, quoted in Harrison, "Subduing," 205.

Page 103—*Although ideas similar to that of stewardship*   Cf. Robin Attfield, *The Ethics of Environmental Concern* (New York: Columbia University Press), 1983, chapter 3; and René Dubos, "Franciscan Conservation versus Benedictine Stewardship," in Berry (ed.), *Environmental Stewardship*, 56–59. Santmire also discusses ideas similar to that of "stewardship" in Augustine. Cf. *The Travail of Nature*, 64–70.

Page 103—*It was regarded as devastated*   Harrison, *The Bible*, especially 142–143; Harrison, "Subduing," especially 103–104.

Page 103—*The seventeenth-century concept of exercising*   Bauckham has a helpful discussion of the understanding of "stewardship" at the time and how it differs from the dominant contemporary understanding in "Stewardship and Relationship," in

Berry (ed.), *The Care of Creation,* 99–106. Harrison also discusses these concepts at length in "Subduing."

Page 103—*Matthew Hale, the chief justice of England*   Matthew Hale, *The Primitive Origination of Mankind* (London: William Godbid), 1677, quoted in Berry (ed.), *The Care of Creation,* 190–91.

Page 104—*As one author wrote*   Flavell, *Husbandry Spiritualized,* Epistle Dedicatory, Sig. A2v, quoted in Harrison, "Subduing," 104.

Page 104—*As philosopher John Locke explained*   Locke, *Two Treatises,* II.v.32, quoted in Harrison, "'Fill the Earth and Subdue It': Biblical Warrants for Colonization in Seventeenth Century England," 20.

Page 104—*E. Calvin Beisner, a professor at Covenant College*   Beisner, *Where Garden Meets Wilderness,* 126, 13. That seventeenth-century stewards, Beisner, and others can believe the earth will be redeemed at the end of time and see that belief as a motivation for the aggressive intervention in (and many today would say destruction of) nature demonstrates that the expectation of the renewal of all things is insufficient to fund an ecologically sensitive faith. N. T. Wright's recent book *Surprised by Hope: Rethinking Heaven, the Resurrection, and the Mission of the Church* (New York: HarperOne, 2008), in which he holds up the prospect of the renewal of all things as self-evidently connected with caring for creation and a progressive social program, may be critiqued for failing to account for this. What matters is not only (or perhaps, not even) believing that the world will be renewed (versus destroyed) at the end of time but the ultimate goal we believe humans should work for to anticipate that redemption, whether that be controlling our passions via reason (church fathers), regaining encyclopedic knowledge (medievals), reordering the natural world (modern stewards), or living in harmony with pregiven states in nature (contemporary stewards).

Page 105—*"There is only one legitimate answer"*   *Christian Century,* November 22, 1950. Palmer discusses these statements and this history in "Stewardship," in *Environmental Stewardship,* 66.

Page 105—*And in 1967, historian Lynn White*   Lynn White, "The Historical Roots of Our Ecological Crisis," *Science* 155, no. 3767 (March 10, 1967): 1203–1207.

Page 106—*As Palmer argues*   Palmer, "Stewardship," in *Environmental Stewardship,* 66–67.

Page 106—*With this new understanding, "environmental stewardship"*   This contrast is helpfully discussed in Bauckham, "Stewardship and Relationship," in Berry (ed.), *The Care of Creation.*

Page 106—*In 1970, the National Association of Evangelicals*   Available at http://www.nae.net/government-affairs/policy-resolutions/132-ecology-1970.

Page 107—Christianity Today *decried*   "Christians and the Pollution Crisis," *Moody Monthly* 71, no. 1 (September 1970): 18–21; "What's Your EQ?" *Christian Life* 33, no. 3 (July 1971): 20–21, 41–42; "Terracide," *Christianity Today* 17, no. 2 (October 26, 1973): 47; "Ecological Phonies," *Christianity Today* 17, no. 2 (October 26, 1973): 47. I get these references from Jared A. Farley, who documents this shift in "The Politicization of the American Evangelical Press, 1960–1981," accessed April 30, 2009;   http://www.ohiolink.edu/etd/view.cgi?acc_num=miami1152903812. See 119 for a discussion of environmentalism.

Page 107—*By 1973,* Christianity Today *was showing*   Editor, "To Live Is to Pollute"; Edith Schaeffer, "Most Dangerous Pollution of All," cited in Fowler, *The Greening of Protestant Thought,* 17–18, 81.

Page 107—*According to a 1978 piece*   "From the Editor," *Christian Life* 40, no. 1 (May 1978): 8. Quoted in Farley, "Politicization," 119.

Page 107—*Over the 1977–78 school year, Calvin College*   Loren Wilkinson. *Earthkeeping: Christian Stewardship of Natural Resources* (Grand Rapids: Wm. B. Eerdmans, 1980).

Page 107—*The Au Sable Institute, an evangelical*   The document can be found in Berry (ed.), *Care of Creation,* 18–22. For a discussion of these trends, see Beisner, *Where Garden Meets Wilderness,* 3–7; Fowler, *The Greening of Protestant Thought,* 76–90.

Page 107—*R. J. Berry, for example, writes about*   Berry (ed.), *The Care of Creation,* 17.

Page 108—*Richard Cizik, for example, writes*   Richard Cizik, "New Moral Awakening, or How I Changed My Mind," in *Yale Divinity School Reflections,* 94(1): 58–60, 2007.

Page 108—*Likewise, Steven Bouma-Prediger*   Steven Bouma-Prediger, *For the Beauty of the Earth: A Christian Vision for Creation Care* (Grand Rapids: Baker Academic, 2001), 90.

Page 109—*Harvard Medical School's Eric Chivian*   Available at http://chge.med.harvard.edu/programs/unite/documents/EricChivian.pdf.

CHAPTER FIVE: EVOLVING EVANGELICALS

Page 111—*"We wished to awaken"*   quoted in Michel Foucault, "Nietzsche, Genealogy, History" in Michel Foucault and Paul Rabinow, *The Foucault Reader* (New York: Vintage, 1984), 79.

Page 111—*As we read in the infamous "Wedge Document"*   Accessed November 18, 2008, http://www.antievolution.org/features/wedge.html.

Page 112—*Similar convictions are artfully expressed*   Cf. John Morris, *The Young Earth: The Real History of the Earth—Past, Present, and Future* (Green Forest: Master Books, 2007).

Page 113—*Neil Shubin, a paleontologist at the University of Chicago*   The entire story of Shubin's trips can be found in Neil Shubin, *Finding Your Inner Fish* (Vintage Books: New York, 2008). See also Jerry A. Coyne, *Why Evolution Is True* (New York: Viking, 2009), 35–38; John Noble Wilford, "Fossil Called Missing Link from Sea to Land Animals," *New York Times,* April 6, 2006.

Page 114—*But they do exist*   One excellent survey of these finds is in Donald R. Prothero, *Evolution: What the Fossils Say and Why It Matters* (New York: Columbia University Press, 2007). Also see Coyne, *Why Evolution Is True,* especially 39–54.

Page 114—*Genetic information for making*   L. Bejder and B. K. Hall, "Limbs in Whales and Limblessness in Other Vertebrates: Mechanisms of Evolutionary and Developmental Transformation and Loss," *Evolution and Development* 4 (2002): 445–458. I got this reference from Coyne, *Why Evolution Is True,* 260.

Page 114—*The same considerations mean that humans*   Prothero, *Evolution,* 343–347. Coyne, *Why Evolution Is True,* 64–66. For further discussion, cf. J. A. Bar-Maor, K. M. Kesner, and J. K. Kaftori, "Human Tails," *Journal of Bone and Joint Surgery* 62 (1980): 508–510.

Page 115—*The reason that humans, gorillas, and chimps need to consume vitamin C in their diets*   One good discussion of these points can be found in Kenneth R. Miller, *Only a Theory: Evolution and the Battle for America's Soul* (Viking: New York, 2008), see especially 88–110. Also see Coyne, *Why Evolution Is True,* 67.

Page 115—*During my undergraduate days at Calvin College*   The symposium was held at Calvin College on March 13, 2006. The quote is a paraphrase of some remarks that Todd Charles Wood made toward the end of his presentation on his work at the Center for Origins Research.

Page 115—*Creationist Henry Morris explains this mentality best when he writes*   Henry M. Morris, *Biblical Cosmology and Modern Science* (Grand Rapids: Baker Book House, 1970), 32–33.

Page 116—*That alone doesn't make it invalid*   Del Ratzsch makes this point well in *The Battle of Beginnings: Why Neither Side Is Winning the Creation-Evolution Debate* (Downers Grove, IL: InterVarsity Press Academic, 1996).

Page 116—*Kuhn argued*   Thomas Kuhn, *The Structure of Scientific Revolutions* (Chicago: University of Chicago Press, 1962).

Page 117—*As one creationist wrote in the 1970s*   Brand, "A Philosophic Rationale for a Creation-Flood Model," *Origins,* 80.

Page 117—*One of the main arguments of this book*   For a discussion of how the critique of foundationalism in science was inspired, in part, by a critique of foundationalism in biblical interpretation (made by a Jesuit priest attacking the Protestant maxim *sola scriptura*), see Princeton philosopher of science Bas van Fraasen, *The Empirical Stance* (New Haven: Yale University Press, 2002), 117–139. Further discussion of the implications of the demise of foundationalism for biblical interpretation and theorizing in general can be found in: Vern S. Poythress, *Science and Hermeneutics: Implications of Scientific Method for Biblical Interpretation* (Grand Rapids: Zondervan, 1988); Nancey Murphy, *Beyond Liberalism and Fundamentalism: How Modern and Postmodern Philosophy Set the Theological Agenda* (Harrisburg: Trinity Press International, 1996); Nancey Murphy, *Anglo-American Postmodernity: Philosophical Perspectives on Science, Religion, and Ethics* (Boulder: Westview Press, 1997); Myron B. Penner (ed.), *Christianity and the Postmodern Turn* (Grand Rapids: Brazos, 2005); James K. A. Smith, *The Fall of Interpretation: Philosophical Foundations for a Creational Hermeneutic* (Downers Grove, IL: InterVarsity Press, 2000); James K. A. Smith, *Who's Afraid of Postmodernism? Taking Derrida, Lyotard, and Foucault to Church* (Grand Rapids: Baker Academic, 2006); James K. A. Smith, *Introducing Radical Orthodoxy: Mapping a Post-Secular Theology* (Grand Rapids: Baker Academic, 2004); J. Wentzel van Huyssteen, *Essays in Post-foundationalist Theology* (Grand Rapids: Wm. B. Eerdmans, 1997); J. Wentzel van Huyssteen, *The Shaping of Rationality: Toward Interdisciplinarity in Theology and Science* (Grand Rapids: Wm. B. Eerdmans, 1999); Merold Westphal (ed.), *Postmodern Philosophy and Christian Thought* (Bloomington: Indiana University Press, 1999); Stanley J. Grenz and John R. Franke, *Beyond Foundationalism: Shaping Theology in a Postmodern Context* (Louisville: Westminster John Knox Press, 2001); John R. Franke, *The Character of Theology: A Postconservative Evangelical Approach: An Introduction to Its Nature, Task, and Purpose* (Grand Rapids: Baker Academic, 2005); Roger E. Olson, *Reformed and Always Reforming: The Postconservative Approach to Evangelical Theology* (Grand Rapids: Baker Academic, 2007); Walter Brueggemann, *Texts Under Negotiation: The Bible and Postmodern Imagination* (Minneapolis: Fortress Press, 1993); Kevin J. Vanhoozer (ed.), *The Cambridge Companion to Postmodern Theology* (Cambridge: Cambridge University Press, 2003); Stanley Hauerwas,

Unleashing Scripture: Freeing the Bible from Its Captivity to America (Nashville: Abinguvnton Press, 1993); Dale B. Martin, *Sex and the Single Savior: Gender and Sexuality in Biblical Interpretation* (Louisville: Westminster John Knox, 2006); Dale B. Martin, *Pedagogy of the Bible: An Analysis and Proposal* (Louisville: Westminster John Knox, 2008); A. K. M. Adam, *Faithful Interpretation: Reading the Bible in a Postmodern World* (Minneapolis: Fortress Press, 2006); A. K. M. Adam, *What Is Postmodern Biblical Criticism?* (Minneapolis: Fortress Press, 1995); The Bible and Culture Collective, *The Postmodern Bible* (New Haven: Yale University Press, 1995); Alasdair MacIntyre, *Three Rival Versions of Moral Enquiry: Encyclopaedia, Genealogy, and Tradition* (Notre Dame: University of Notre Dame Press); Imre Lakatos, "Science and Pseudoscience," in *Philosophy of Science: The Central Issues* (New York: W. W. Norton & Company, 1998); Stanley Fish, *Is There a Text in This Class? The Authority of Interpretive Communities* (Cambridge: Harvard University Press, 1980).

Page 117—*In the process, we will see that creationism*   My claim is not that no past interpretations of Genesis were similar to those of creationists or that the human author did not intend to say any of the things that creationists take him as saying but rather that the interpretive framework creationists bring to Genesis represents a break in many ways with the interpretive framework past Christians brought to it (which included elements that would have likely prevented them from interpreting it in a creationist manner in light of our contemporary scientific knowledge). I'm more interested in interpretive frameworks in this history than in interpretations.

Page 117—*"The proposition that the Bible"*   Charles Hodge, "The Bible in Science," *New York Observer,* March 26, 1863. Quoted in Noll, *Scandal of the Evangelical Mind,* 183–184.

Page 118—*"We know [God] in two manners"*   "Belgic Confession," in Alister McGrath (ed.), *The Christian Theology Reader,* 2nd ed. (Oxford: Blackwell Publishing Ltd, 2001), 104.

Page 118—*As creationist Henry Morris puts it*   Henry Morris, "The Bible *Is* a Textbook of Science" (1964–1965), *Studies in the Bible and Science,* 114, cited in George M. Marsden, *Understanding Fundamentalism and Evangelicalism* (Grand Rapids: Wm. B. Eerdmans, 1991), 158.

Page 118—*Likewise, John Morris writes*   Morris, *The Young Earth,* 32–34.

Page 119—*The early Christians strongly sensed*   Cf. Bart Ehrman, *Lost Christianities: The Battle for Scripture and the Faiths We Never Knew* (New York: Oxford University Press, 2003); Robert M. Grand and David Tracy, *A Short History of the Interpreta-*

tion of the Bible (Minneapolis: Fortress Press, 1963), see especially 73–82; Kathryn Greene-McCreight, *Ad Litteram: How Augustine, Calvin, and Barth Read the "Plain Sense" of Genesis 1–3* (New York: Peter Lang Publishing Inc., 1999); Dale B. Martin, *Sex and the Single Savior: Gender and Sexuality in Biblical Interpretation* (Louisville: Westminster John Knox, 2006), 4–5; Anthony C. Thiselton, *New Horizons in Hermeneutics: The Theory and Practice of Transforming Biblical Reading* (Grand Rapids: Zondervan, 1992), 142–178.

Page 119—*As Augustine put it*   Augustine, *Literal Meaning of Genesis,* 2.6.12. Quoted in Greene-McCreight, *Ad Litteram,* 48.

Page 119—*Or as John Calvin put it*   John Calvin, *Commentaries on the First Book of Moses Called Genesis,* trans. John King, 1:86–87. Quoted in Ibid.

Page 120—*Calvin explains this apparent inconsistency*   Discussed in Greene-McCreight, *Ad Litteram,* 129.

Page 120—*Each passage*   Greene-McCreight, *Ad Litteram,* 48.

Page 121—*As Augustine put it, "[A]nything in the divine discourse"*   Augustine, *Christian Doctrine,* 3.33–34.

Page 121—*In his allegorical interpretation of Genesis*   Augustine, *Confessions*, 12–13. My discussion of Augustine's interpretation is informed by Dale B. Martin's summary and analysis in *Pedagogy of the Bible: An Analysis and Proposal* (Louisville: Westminster John Knox, 2008), 56–60.

Page 121—*Augustine ends this exposition*   Augustine, *Confessions,* 12.25.35. Quoted in Martin, *Pedagogy of the Bible,* 58.

Page 122—*he insists on multiple interpretations*   Ibid., 13.24.36. Quoted in Ibid., 59.

Page 122—*Oxford's Peter Harrison explains*   Peter Harrison, *The Bible, Protestantism and the Rise of Natural Science* (Cambridge: Cambridge University Press, 1998), 122. This whole shift is discussed in pages 64–160. See also Hans Frei, *The Eclipse of Biblical Narrative: A Study in Eighteenth and Nineteenth Century Hermeneutics* (New Haven: Yale University Press, 1974).

Page 123—*Harrison explains, "these narratives"*   Harrison, *The Bible*, 129.

Page 123—*Questions shifted from the potential theological significance*   Ibid., 128.

Page 123—*Scripture may be another source of facts about nature and the past*   Ibid., 126.

Page 124—*One theologian at the time noted*   Quoted in ibid., 127.

Page 124—*One Cambridge University professor*   Quoted in ibid., 139–140.

Page 124—*It was in this context that the flood of Noah*   Cf. David Livingstone, *Darwin's Forgotten Defenders: The Encounter Between Evangelical Theology and Evolutionary Thought* (Grand Rapids: Wm. B. Eerdmans, 1987); Prothero, *What the Fossils Say*, 28–29,

58–78, 87–88. Harlow also notes this in "The Genesis Creation Accounts." "Readers of Genesis have been tempted for centuries to take the life spans of the figures recorded in the genealogies, crunch the numbers, and come up with a date for the creation of the earth and, indeed, the universe. The first person to do this in a way that became widely influential in Western culture was Archbishop James Ussher, the primate of Ireland, who lived 1581–1656. He proposed that the first day of creation was Sunday, October 23, 4004 B.C.E., a date that would make the universe about six thousand years old. A contemporary of Ussher's, John Lightfoot of Cambridge, narrowed the moment of creation even further, to 9:00 a.m. on the same date" (30–31).

Page 124—*Henry Morris, speaking of the Bible, writes of*   Quoted in Marsden, *Understanding Fundamentalism and Evangelicalism*, 163.

Page 124—*And in an age in which "science" was*   Noll, *Scandal*, 83–108.

Page 125—*Drawing on the two books doctrine*   Rodney L. Stiling, "Scriptural Geology in America," in *Evangelicals and Science in Historical Perspective* (New York: Oxford University Press, 1999), 177–192. The quote is from page 179.

Page 125—*America's top geologists, who were mostly evangelical*   Ibid.

Page 125—*In the 1820s, these authors*   Ibid.

Page 126—*White's writing is held at the same level*   Livingstone, *Darwin's Forgotten Defenders,* 157; Ronald L. Numbers, "Creating Creationism: Meanings and Uses since the Age of Agassiz," in David M. Livingstone, D. G. Hart, and Mark A. Noll (eds.), *Evangelicals and Science in Historical Perspective* (New York: Oxford University Press, 1999), 234–243. The quote is from page 237; Numbers, *The Creationists*. I should note here that, after coming up with the title for this section—"The Creation of Creationism"—I found variations on it in many of my sources. I don't cite these because it is a fairly common word-play and I don't know who originally came up with it.

Page 126—*Indeed, the writing of the scriptural geologists*   Stiling, "Scriptural Geology," in Livingstone, Hart, and Noll (eds.), *Evangelicals and Science*, 177–192.

Page 126—*This shift was so thorough, that, as one author notes*   Del Ratzsch, *The Battle of Beginnings*, 56.

Page 126—*The new biblical interpretations forged by mainstream*   Stiling, "Scriptural Geology," in Livingstone, Hart, and Noll (eds.), *Evangelicals and Science,* 186.

Page 126—*"I do not think that there is any"*   Quoted in Livingstone, *Darwin's Forgotten Defenders*, 118.

Page 127—*"would have been a precursor of the modern evolutionary theorists"*   Quoted in ibid., 120.

Page 127—*"there is a theistic and an atheistic"*   Quoted in ibid., 105.

Page 127—*The fundamentalist movement arose*   Cf. Noll, *Between Faith and Criticism*; Ratzsch, *Battle of the Beginnings,* 55–67.

Page 128—*George Frederick Wright, a theologian and geologist*   Both Wright and Orr quotations are from Livingstone, *Darwin's Forgotten Defenders,* 142, 150.

Page 128—*Two other authors*   Quoted in ibid., 154, 153.

Page 128—*While the early fundamentalist movement embraced*   George M. Marsden, "Why Creation Science?," in *Understanding Fundamentalism and Evangelicalism* (Grand Rapids: Wm. B. Eerdmans, 1991), 153–181.

Page 129—*Notre Dame historian George Marsden explains*   Marsden, *Understanding Fundamentalism and Evangelicalism,* 165.

Page 129—*Thus, in the words of one early fundamentalist*   Quoted in ibid.

Page 129—*This mind-set is well illustrated by a cartoon*   Morris, *Young Earth,* 35.

Page 130—*R. A. Torrey, a chief editor*   Quoted in Livingstone, *Darwin's Forgotten Defenders*, 151.

Page 130—*Another popular strategy was to suggest*   Quoted in Numbers, *The Creationists*, 128.

Page 130—*Indeed, it turns out that, for most of the first half of the twentieth century*   Livingstone, *Darwin's Forgotten Defenders*, 157–158; Numbers, *The Creationists*, 88–120.

Page 131—*Ellen G. White's divinely inspired interpretation of Genesis*   Numbers, *The Creationists*, 8; Numbers, "Creationism in 20th-Century America"; Ratzsch, *Battle of the Beginnings,* 65.

Page 131—*The proponents of creationism*   Numbers, "Creationism in 20th-Century America"; Geisler, *The Creator in the Courtroom: Scopes II.*

Page 132—*Mark Noll puts it best when he notes*   Noll, *Scandal of the Evangelical Mind,* 199.

Page 133—*"I hold to a historical grammatical hermeneutic"*   Morris, *Young Earth,* 30.

Page 133—*And many serious biblical scholars*   Thus, James Barr, a leading expert on the Hebrew Bible from Vanderbilt University, can declare, "so far as I know there is no professor of Hebrew or Old Testament at any world-class university who does not believe that the writer(s) of *Genesis* 1–11 intended to convey to their readers . . . [that] creation took place in a series of six days which were the same as the days of 24 hours we now experience." Alvin Plantinga makes this point in

"Evolution, Neutrality, and Antecedent Probability," in Robert T. Pennock (ed.), *Intelligent Design Creationism and Its Critics: Philosophical, Theological, and Scientific Perspectives*, 197–236. Also cf. Daniel C. Harlow, "Creation According to Genesis: Literary Genre, Cultural Context, Theological Truth," in *Christian Scholar's Review* 37, no. 2 (2008): 163–198. Harlow's article was very helpful in the discussion below.

Page 133—*So what's the problem?* The points in this paragraph and those that follow are heavily indebted to Harlow, "Creation According to Genesis."

Page 134—*And when the flood of Noah occurred* For an interesting discussion of how the church fathers interpreted these passages, see Stanley L. Jaki, *Genesis 1 Through the Ages* (London: Thomas More Press, 1992), 70–108. One of the central debates of the church fathers was just how all that water could remain on top of the sky dome. "Whatever the nature of that water and whatever the manner of its being there," Augustine wrote, "we must not doubt that it does exist in that place." And at any rate, Augustine continued, we do know that the firmament "constitutes an impassable boundary between the waters above and the waters below" (93–94).

Page 134—*Henry Morris, for example, draws on knowledge of modern science* Henry M. Morris, *Biblical Creationism: What Each Book of the Bible Teaches About Creation and the Flood* (Grand Rapids: Baker Book House, 1993), 20. This is ironic since Morris elsewhere states, "We should read and believe it exactly as it stands, without trying to 'interpret' it to fit some theory of men," 18.

Page 135—*"When the Bible speaks of the foundations"* Charles Hodge, "The Bible in Science," *New York Observer*, March 26, 1863.

Page 135—*Ancient people not only lived on a flat earth* The interpretation in this paragraph is informed by Harlow, "The Genesis Creation Accounts," *Christian Scholar's Review*; Jaki, *Genesis 1 Through the Ages*; and Greene-McCreight, *How Augustine, Calvin, and Barth Read the "Plain Sense" of Genesis 1–3*.

Page 136—*The evolution of creationism* See Miller, *Only a Theory*, 111–134 for a discussion of the incident. The quote is from 116.

Page 137—*Intelligent design advocates say* Phillip E. Johnson, *Darwin on Trial* (Downers Grove, IL: InterVarsity Press, 1993), 19. Francis S. Collins, *The Language of God: A Scientist Presents Evidence for Belief* (New York: Free Press, 2006).

Page 138—*In humans, for example, about sixty new mutations* Collins, *Language of God*, 131.

Page 138—*Some mutations, for example, have given prostitutes*   Cf. S. L. Rowland-Jones et al., "Cytotoxic T Cell Responses to Multiple Conserved HIV Epitopes in HIV-Resistant Prostitutes in Nairobi," *Journal of Clinical Investigation* 102, no. 9 (1998): 1758–1765.

Page 138—*Nylon was invented in 1935*   Miller, *Only a Theory*, 79–84. Miller's discussion is based on a discussion available at http://www.ccrnp.ncifcrf.gov/~toms/paper/ev/ and also Irfan D. Prijambada et al., "Emergence of Nylon through Oligomer Degradation Enzymes in *Pseudomonas aeruginosa* PAO Through Experimental Evolution," *Applied and Environmental Microbiology* 61 (1995): 2020–2022.

Page 139—*Duplicate a few genes there*   This is not meant to give a precise formula from moving from one genome to the other, of course, but simply to point out that the difference between species results from specific, identifiable differences in genomes, not mystical categories of "forms" or other such boundaries.

Page 139—*The rate of such mutations is well known*   Cf. D. Reznick et al., "Evaluation of the Rate of Evolution in Natural Populations of Guppies (*Poecilia reticulata*)," *Science* 275 (1997): 1934–1936, cited in Miller, *Finding Darwin's God*, 107–111.

Page 139—*Behe's 1996 book*   Michael J. Behe, *Darwin's Black Box: The Biochemical Challenge to Evolution* (New York: Free Press, 1996).

Page 139—*"Darwin's Demise"*   *Biola Connections*, Summer 2003, accessed May 1, 2009, http://www.biola.edu/news/biolamag/downloads/Summer_2003.pdf.

Page 139—Christianity Today *even gave Behe*   "1997 Book Awards," *Christianity Today*, April 28, 1997, accessed May 1, 2009, http://www.google.com/search?rlz=1C1CHMA_enUS320US320&sourceid=chrome&ie=UTF-8&q=7t5012.

Page 141—*"arise as an integrated unit"*   Behe, *Darwin's Black Box*, 39.

Page 142—*Indeed, as scientists have shown*   Cf. W. F. Doolittle and O. Zhaxbayeva, "Evolution: Reducible Complexity—the Case for Bacterial Flagella," *Current Biology* 17 (2007): R510-R512; M. J. Pallen and N. J. Matzke, "From *The Origin of Species* to the Origin of Bacterial Flagella," *Nature Reviews Microbiology* 4 (2006): 784–790; E. Meléndez-Hevia, T. G. Waddell, and M. Cascante, "The Puzzle of the Krebs Citric Acid Cycle: Assembling the Pieces of Chemically Feasible Reactions, and Opportunism in the Design of Metabolic Pathways During Evolution," *Journal of Molecular Evolution* 43 (1996): 293; Y. Jiang and R. F. Doolittle, "The Evolution of Vertebrate Blood Coagulation as Viewed from a Comparison of Puffer Fish and Sea Squirt Genomes," *Proceedings of the National Academy of Sciences of the United States of America* 100 (2003): 7527–7532; S. M. Musser and S. I. Chan, "Evolution of the Cytochrome C Oxidase Proton Pump," *Journal of Molecular Evolution* 46 (1998): 508–520.

Page 142—*The only thing necessary for a system to evolve*   Probably the best scientific critic of intelligent design is Brown University's Kenneth R. Miller, himself a theologically conservative Roman Catholic. Cf. *Finding Darwin's God* and *Only a Theory*, as well as his "The Flagellum Unspun: The Collapse of Irreducible Complexity," in *Debating Design: From Darwin to DNA* (Cambridge University Press, 2004), 81–97.

Page 143—*Behe himself, in his 2008 book* The Edge of Evolution   Michael Behe, *The Edge of Evolution: The Search for the Limits of Darwinism* (New York: Free Press, 2007), 237. I initially encountered this quote on http://darwinianconservatism. blogspot.com/2008/05/has-michael-behe-fallen-from-favor-at.html. Accessed on September 20, 2010.

Page 144—*"Maybe the designer* isn't *all"*   Behe, *Edge of Evolution*, 239.

Page 144—*As philosopher Stanley Fish puts it*   Perhaps the best critique of the "keep an open mind" argument is by the theorist Stanley Fish in "Academic Cross-Dressing: How Intelligent Design Gets Its Arguments from the Left," in *Harper's Magazine* 70, no. 3 (December 2005): 311.

Page 145—*After Nancey Murphy, a philosopher of science*   Shankar Vendantam, "Eden and Evolution," in *The Washington Post*, February 5, 2006, W08, accessed June 13, 2009, http://www.washingtonpost.com/wp-dyn/content/article/2006/02/03/AR2006020300822_pf.html.

Page 145—*Does it really matter that*   Cited in Numbers, *The Creationists*, 1.

Page 146—*The evangelical campaign against embryonic stem cell research*   For a survey of this movement, see Chris Mooney, *The Republican War on Science* (New York: Basic Books, 2005). For a discussion of Prentice and stem cells, see for example: Shane Smith, William Neaves, and Steven Teitelbaum, "Adult Stem Cell Treatments for Diseases?," *Science* 313 (July 28, 2006): 439; David A. Prentice and Gene Tarne, "Treating Diseases with Adult Stem Cells," *Science* 315 (January 19, 2007) 328; Shane Smith, William Neaves, and Steven Teitelbaum, "Adult Versus Embryonic Stem Cells: Treatments," *Science* 316 (June 8, 2007) 1422; David A. Prentice and Gene Tarne, "Adult Versus Embryonic Stem Cells: Treatments," ibid.; and Robert S. Schwartz, "The Politics and Promise of Stem-Cell Research," *New England Journal of Medicine* 355 (2006): 1189–1191.

Page 146—*Evangelical antienvironmentalism*   Beisner, *Where Garden Meets Wilderness*.

Page 147—*And the evangelical campaign against homosexuality*   See Chapter 3. Kenneth Miller makes a similar argument in *Only a Theory.*

Epilogue: Neo-Neo-Evangelicalism

Page 149—*So this group of Christians decided*   Excellent overviews of this history can be found in Smith, *American Evangelicalism,* 13–15; Marsden, *Understanding Fundamentalism and Evangelicalism*, 62–82.

INDEX

ABOUT THE AUTHOR

Jonathan Dudley is a graduate of Calvin College (BS, biology) and Yale Divinity School (MA, ethics) and is currently an MD student at the Johns Hopkins School of Medicine. He has worked to provide medical care to underserved Hispanic populations in Grand Rapids, Michigan; Guatemala; and Ecuador, and has also worked as an ethical consultant for the National Institute on Drug Abuse. This book began as a column series in the *Yale Daily News*.